Bath & Spa

Bath

Sibylle Kramer

& Spa

BRAUN

CONTENTS

Bath & Spa
by Sibylle Kramer

There are social trends that are quickly reflected in the prevailing architectural style. The new joy of cooking, for example, has led to kitchens being increasingly designed as open spaces today. Within the past few years, a rethinking process took place in this area that substantially altered the view of a functional part of the home. In the bathroom sector a similar trend seems to be taking place that is expected to increase in the near future. The interesting aspect of this trend is the correlation between public and private bathing areas. This is mainly the reason why the fashionable term SPA has become the synonym for restorative relaxation – increasingly also in the privacy of the home.

However, the frequently stated belief that the word spa is a Latin acronym – sanus per aquam (health through water) – is only an illusion since neither the sources nor the rules of Latin grammar support such a conclusion. Instead the symbolic value of the word actually derives from the Belgian bathing resort of Spa, which was already frequented by British tourists in the 16th century. Yet antiquity is an interesting starting point for studying the culture of bathing. The Roman Thermae were public places and water a precious commodity that was fetched via aqueducts. The link between hygiene and sufficient water supply was one of the basic pillars of the imperium romanum.

In the Middle Ages, public bath houses were the place in which most people came in contact with running water. Crusaders had brought the concept and the construction plans along with them from the Middle East. However, religious prudery, the spread of syphilis and, last but not least, the great bubonic plague epidemics resulted in the shutting down of most bath houses. From then on, especially among feudal circles, personal hygiene was reduced to the use of perfumes.

It was not until the 19th century that new hygienic insights led to a revival of public baths. This was followed by the increased privatization of baths. Gaining in strength, the bourgeoisie added bathrooms as a representative architectural element to their homes, creating a new functional room. Until the period of promoterism many urban houses at least featured a common bathroom in the hallway. Individualization progressed as people were now eager to construct a separate bathroom in each residential unit. Those who had plenty of space at their disposal even managed to install a guest toilet or guest bathroom. This progressed into the assignment of separate bathing areas to each person in the household, where possible. Whether the efforts include installing master bathrooms, parent and children bathrooms or simple dual bathroom sinks, all have one aim in common – turning the bathroom into an individual area of expression and retreat. This way, in its architectural evolution from a public to a private space, the bathroom developed into the perfect symbol of cocooning.

As a result of the recent wellness movement, an exciting observation can be made at this point. Increasingly, public bathing institutions that for a long time only drudged along as boring swimming halls are gaining in popularity. Spruced up by architects and designers, they shine as new spa temples that not only revive the ritual character of bathing

during antiquity but also include Middle Eastern and oriental influences. This way, they not only define a new public function for the bathing space but also act as ideals and models for the design of many private bathrooms.

Bathrooms in homes increasingly feature an open design while the choice of materials has expanded. The bathroom as a space is given more importance in the planning stage. Previously, bathrooms were frequently located on the interior, while today daylight illumination is almost compulsory. The number of manufacturers of bathroom furniture, faucets and ceramics is also constantly increasing. New materials and manufacturing techniques allow, for example, the use of tiles with unusual dimensions or sinks made of composite materials that can be molded in any shape. This way, they once again constitute cultic vessels for the matter whose specific characteristics enable life on earth – water. At 0° Celsius it turns into ice, at 4° it reaches its highest liquid density – a characteristics that not only ensures the survival of fish. Hot-blooded, our body temperature is around 37°, and finally at 100°, water evaporates into steam.

The chapters of this book take readers along these important temperature points, introducing architectural environ-

ments that emerge at the meeting point of the solid and liquid shape. A total of 67 international projects invite readers of this book to discover the connection and interaction between public spas and private bathrooms and to envision their very own wellness wonderland.

0°

Matteo Thun

↑ | **Winter fairy tale,** outdoor back fence
→ | **Vigilius,** swimming pool with view

Vigilius Mountain Resort
Lana

The hotel can only be reached by cable car or by foot. The new building section stretching from north to south consists of two floors above the ground and one below it. The structure is fitted into the natural hilly landscape and acts as an extended contour of its surroundings, an effect generated by a planted, accessible roof. The desire to integrate the hotel complex into nature is expressed in the "paradise garden"– a small green hill grown with larch trees that is located in the central part of the building, between the guest rooms and the spa. This area stimulates the meditative understanding of nature. The project employs traditional building materials such as rock, wood, clay and glass, while large windows enable the optimal use of solar energy to maintain a positive balance of energy.

PROJECT FACTS **Address:** Vigiljoch, Lana, Italy. **Builder-owner:** private. **Completion:** 2003. **Total area:** 14,000 m². **Hotel area:** 11,500 m². **Gross volume:** 17,300 m³.

↑ | **Exterior view,** sun-bathing terrace
← | **Façade,** eastern side

↑ | **Interior view,** swimming pool
← | **Room interior,** bathroom

↑ I **Bathroom,** Nighthawk
→ I **Interior,** small bathroom

Nighthawk, Startrek and Large Scene
Visions for Alape

The three designs by London designer Yorgo Lykouria deal with the concept of the bathroom of the future. He skillfully integrates formal elements from the realm of science fiction movies, while the futuristic paradigms are also present in the technical implementation details. These include, for example, sensors for the doors and the lighting. He describes the bathroom also as a place where one can enjoy different experiences and emotions and in which not only the body but the soul has a chance to retreat and cleanse itself.

Client: Alape GmbH, Am Gräbicht 1–9, 38644 Goslar, Germany.

←↙ | **Large Scene,** bathroom showroom for Alape
↓ | **Bathroom,** Startrek

Zaha Hadid

↑ | **Interior view,** hotel room
→ | **Bathroom,** single surface design concept

Hotel Puerta America, Level 1
Madrid

The hotel development comprises 14 floors in total which 14 designers have been commissioned to design one floor each. Hadid's response to the clichéd hotel bedroom is to develop a new dialogue between the complex and continuous nature of merging forms and textures. This seamless fluidity represents a new language of domestic architecture – created by new developments in digital design and enhanced manufacturing capabilities. Inside the rooms, the floor, wall and furniture constitute one continuous surface or skin, making them pieces of art. Every single element, whether the walls, bedroom door with its LED signs, sliding door to the bathroom, bathtub or vanity unit, is rounded in a single curved sweep.

PROJECT FACTS

Address: Avenida de América 41, 28002 Madrid, Spain. **Builder-owner:** Grupo Urvasco. **Completion:** 12.2004. **Area:** 1,200 m². **Project team:** Woody K T Yao, Patrik Schumacher, Thomas Vietzke, Yael Brosilovski, Mirco Becker, Ken Bostock. **Project manager (local):** Luis Leon – Castellana 2000.

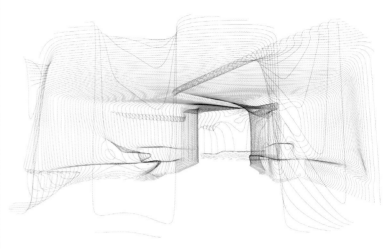

←←| **Solid surface,** fluid forms, material
LG_Himacs
← | **Interior view,** corridor
↑ | **Rendering**
↓ | **Interior view,** lobby

Stefan Ghetta | Schletterer
Wellness & Spa Design

↑ | **View of the Zugspitze mountain,** glass
façade (1,200 m²)
↗ | **Exterior view,** façade
→ | **Interior view,** colorful play of light

Mohr Life Resort

Lermoos

The 1,800 m² resort is a comfortable rendering of modern architecture. Comfortable materials create a homelike atmosphere which is why the hotel never seems cold and imper-
sonal. Yet the traditional materials were interpreted in a modern way, not only optically
but also in terms of room climate. The elements contrast with one another – the pool is
completely submerged in RGB light, while the glass façade, measuring more than 1,200 m²,
offers a unobstructed view of the Zugspitze mountain.

PROJECT FACTS

Address: Hotel Mohr Life Resort, Innsbruckerstrasse 40, 6631 Lermoos, Austria. **Builder-owner:** Klaus Mantl and Tina Künstner Mantl. **Completion:** 12.2006. **Area:** 2,000 m².

↑ | **Detail**
↓ | **Freehand sketch,** trilogy

← | **Exterior view,** brine pool, Zugspitze mountain
↓ | **Interior view,** pool, glass façade

Crepain Binst Architecture
(Jo Crepain)

↑ | **Interior view,** bathroom
↗ | **Bathroom,** view into the shower
→ | **Exterior view,** newly added floors
→→| **Floor plans**

Loft
Antwerp

The building design incorporates offices for up to 60 people from level one to three. Level four consists of a residence for a couple with room for an art collection, roof terrace, master bedroom, bathroom, guestroom and an atelier surrounding the west-facing roof terrace. The living room is four meters high and offers a panoramic view of the city from both the front and the back of the building, overlooking the rooftops of Antwerp. The roof unit was insulated on the outside and clad with smooth aluminum siding. These new building elements light up brightly in the sunlight, in contrast to the old restored façade and the dark gray side and back walls.

PROJECT FACTS

Address: Vlaanderenstraat 6, 2000 Antwerp, Belgium. **Builder-owner:** Family Crepain. **Construction time:** 1995–1997. **Total floor area residence:** 340 m². **Interior designer:** Jo Crepain, Maarten van Severen, Nadia Pelckmans. **General contractor:** Van Rymenant nv.

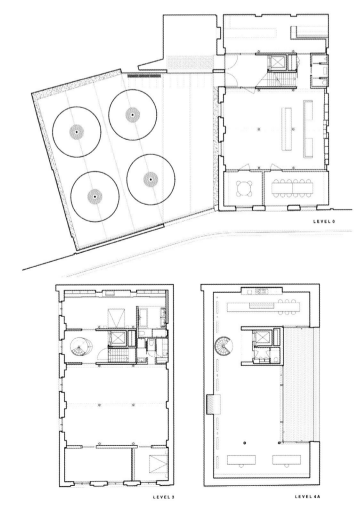

LEVEL 0

LEVEL 3

LEVEL 4A

Loodszeven
Interieurarchitecten

↖ | **Floor and wall,** grey Chinese basalt stone
↑ | **Washbasin,** Marike, glacier white
→ | **Glass panel,** grey colored translucent foil

Private Bathroom
Amsterdam

This very small bathroom has been designed with the freedom of not having to place a bathtub. This resulted in a somewhat more spacious layout. All materials were selected to create a natural, powerful, modern, yet warm look. Big gestures were made to achieve maximum impact, at the same time providing a certian soberness and minimalism. Chinese basalt stone was cut in sleights up to 1800/500 mm in width, while the mirror was kept as big as possible to give an impression of spaciousness. As a contrast to all of this, small strips of rust/gold colored Norwegian slate were used on the shower floor. This very exclusive stone has anti slip qualities, looks very natural, and is the primary eye catcher when entering the room.

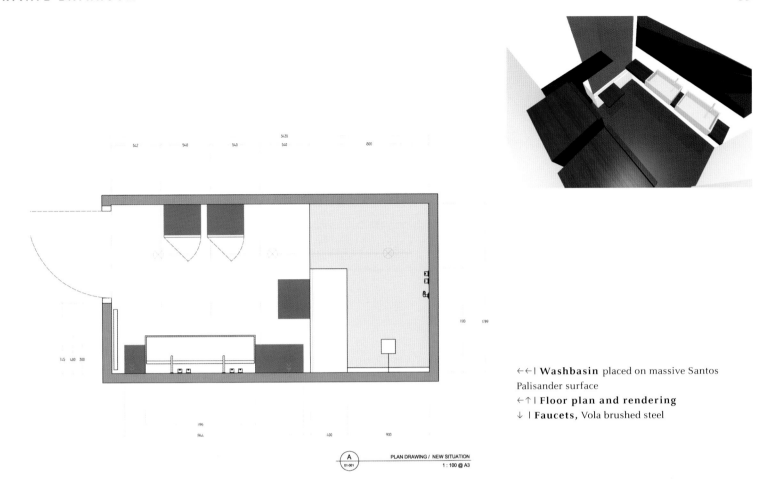

← ← | **Washbasin** placed on massive Santos Palisander surface
← ↑ | **Floor plan and rendering**
↓ | **Faucets,** Vola brushed steel

A
01-001

PLAN DRAWING / NEW SITUATION
1 : 100 @ A3

Architecture Research
Office LLC

↑ | **Flagship store,** exterior view
→ | **Interior,** organza veils in dyed milky white,
aqua, and darker blues

Qiora Store and Spa
New York

The word Qiora, which means "light from within," is the brand name of the holistic skin-care product line launched in 2001 by Japan's Shiseido Cosmetics. ARO was commissioned to design a day spa which would also serve as the brand's flagship store. To combine a spa's need for privacy with the public setting required for successful retail, ARO utilized Qiora's own holistic approach to skin health. If the store and spa are outwardly luminous, the source of such light must be a sense of inner calm, and vice versa.

PROJECT FACTS

Address: Madison Avenue, New York, USA. **Builder-owner:** Shiseido Corporation. **Construction time:** 04.2000–12.2000. **Budget:** $ 1.7 million. **Area:** 1,500 ft².

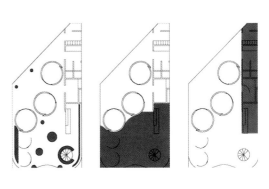

↑ | **Section,** boundaries between luxury and utility
←←| **Sales area,** shelves of frosted acrylic
← | **Early design sketch**
↙ | **Furniture** designed by Shiseido creative director Aoshi Kudo

↑ | **Exterior view,** gabion façade
→ | **Interior view,** bathroom

House 9x9

Stadtbergen

The two-floor home is designed as a habitable sculpture for a couple. Based on the square ground-floor layout of 9x9 meters of the master plan, a two-floor open room sequence with living, dining and kitchen areas on the ground floor and a working gallery, sleeping, dressing and bathroom on the second floor, as well as a reading loft beneath the asymmetrical pyramid roof was developed. The rough exterior of the building is in contrast to the delicately finished, light-colored and bright interior concept. All dimensions of the little house (width, depth, height) can be experienced from different viewing angles, which creates a generous and uncongested overall room impression.

PROJECT FACTS

Address: Maria-Hilf-Strasse 17, 86193 Stadtbergen, Germany. **Builder-owner:** Claus Kaelber and Barbara Gayer. **Construction time:** 10.2002–09.2003. **Construction costs:** approx. € 380,000. **Area:** approx. 128 m². **Gross volume:** approx. 640 m³ (above ground). **Project management:** Szabolcs Sóti, Helmut Schmid. **Model making:** Bettina Stix, Niya Tasheva; Schreinerei Huber, Kissing.

Plan2Plus
Ralf Peter Knobloch
Ursula Regina Förster

↑ | **Washbasin**
↗ | **Lighting,** changing light accentuates the room concept
→ | **Isometry**

LANCÔME Beauty Institute
Munich

The soft edges and open design of the various functional areas generate a harmonious overall picture, which supports the relaxed effect of the special treatments, even incorporating the world of scents. Carefully balanced materials and details, such as polished and silvered elements contrasting with white high gloss furniture, are the basis of the stylish, clear and functional design. Structured wall coverings and textile suspensions, mosaic tiles by Bisazza as well as warm wooden surfaces create visual and palpable contrasts that appeal to the senses. The room-high elements create an open setting for the exclusive beauty institute.

PROJECT FACTS

Address: Karstadt Oberpollinger, Munich, Germany. **Builder-owner:** LANCÔME. **Completion:** 11.2006.
Designer: Plan2Plus architektur innenarchitektur design, Munich. **Planning partner:** Jutta Kniess
(LANCÔME Germany, Diréctrice Grands Magasins).

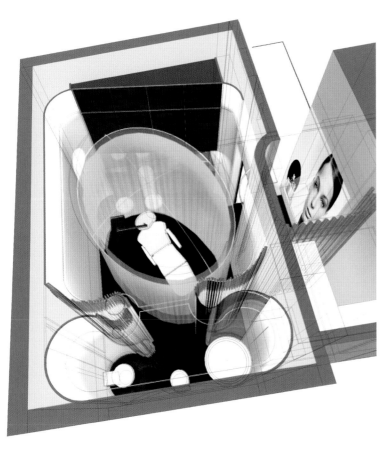

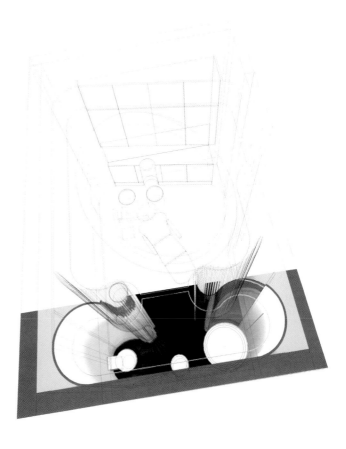

Uwe Bernd Friedemann

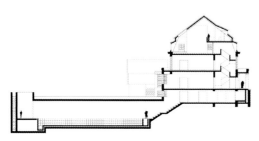

Restructured Villa
Cologne

Initially it was supposed to be only a conversion of the attic. However, soon architect Uwe Bernd Friedemann found himself in the midst of a complete restructuring of a historic villa from the year 1913 located in Cologne. It incorporated not only the living spaces but also an intricate bathroom area, which constituted a direct and courageous commitment to no-frills aesthetics. The choice of materials was limited to white plastered walls, dark gray natural stone and lye-dipped room-length Douglas pine floorboards. The architectural concept is also strongly expressed in the bathroom – a reduction to the essential with a very courageous use of open spaces. A narrow stone stairway leads from the ground floor down to this area, which is distinguished by its architectural clarity and is given an almost sacral air by its intransigent purism.

The bathing area extends below the garden through a newly constructed swimming hall reaching to the end of the property – a 25-meter long swimming lane that is available for exercise. At the end of this tunnel, a room-high glass sliding door measuring 3x4 meters can be slid open by the push of a button to access the garden from the lowered patio. The elevated ground floor of the historic villa includes fitness, relaxation and personal care areas, as well as a Jacuzzi and a Finnish sauna with a view of the garden. Their design is as touchingly simple as that of the whole residence and the premises are additionally distinguished by their encompassing geometry.

↑↑ | **Interior view,** 25-meter long swimming lane
↑ | **Section**
→ | **Bathroom** in plain geometry

PROJECT FACTS Address: Cologne, Germany. **Completion:** 1913, 2001–2003 (conversion). **Original architect:** Herman Pflaume (1913). **Area:** 2,700 m² (total), 1,400 m² (living space), 500 m² (spa).

←←| **Basement,** spa area
← | **View,** sliding door to the patio
↓ | **Floor plan**

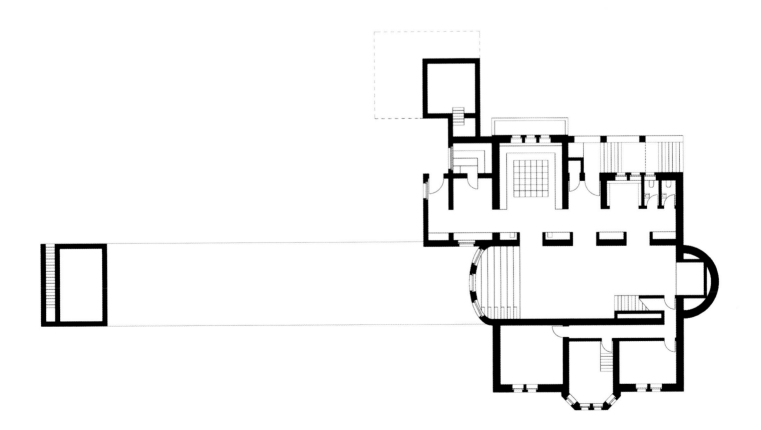

Javier Mariscal &
Fernando Salas

↑ | **Interior view,** hotel room
↓ | **Hotel room,** detail

→ | **Interior view,** hotel room and bathroom are
open and connected with each other

Hotel Puerta America, Level 11
Madrid

The space concept was derived from the need for various functions to share a limited space, including the bedroom, desk, living room and bathroom. In the design process, the bathroom grew until it took over the whole room. This is why the two ceramic surfaces on the bathroom floor and wall extend into the room, expanding the presence of this material. For the same reasons, two types of surfaces surround the washbasin, while the shower provides extensive visual perspectives. Inside the bathroom, the only closed area is the toilet and bidet cubicle, which turns into a huge lamp by backlighting it through an ash wood trellis. The reverse side of the mirror supports the plasma screen TV and is fitted with the Nomad light by Modular as well as the Rifle magnifying mirror by Agape.

Address: Avenida de América 41, 28002 Madrid, Spain. **Builder-owner:** Hoteles Silken. **Construction time:** 2004–2005. **Completion:** 07.2005.

Carl D'Aquino &
Francine Monaco of
D'Aquino Monaco

↑ | **Twin columns,** water creating a "silver rain"
↗ | **Reception area** on a tranquil island
→ | **Entry,** inspired by a Swiss glacier

Silver Rain a La Prairie Spa
at the Ritz Carlton Grand Cayman

Taking their cue from the purity of a Swiss glacier, the designers have created the luxuri-
ous, water-based interiors of the 18,700 ft² Silver Rain a La Prairie Spa. The guests are surrounded by the comforting aura of water in all its states. This unique experience begins
the moment the guests open the silver-leafed doors and enter a quietly dazzling space that
introduces them to the tranquil experience of the spa beyond. Water rushes beneath the
tiled floor and behind screened walls – water that is heard but not yet seen.

PROJECT FACTS
Address: Ritz Carlton, Grand Cayman, Cayman Islands. **Owner / developer:** Michael Ryan, Ritz Carlton Grand Cayman Resort.

49

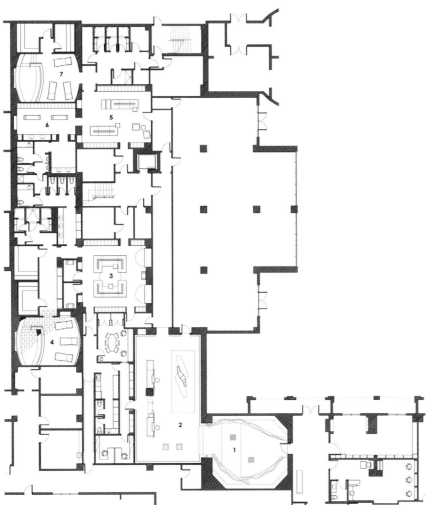

↑ | **Interior view,** personalized seating area
← | **Floor plan**
↗→ | **Lounges,** seating and furnishing custom
designed by D'Aquino Monaco

Giovanni Pagani
Maurizio di Mauro

↑ | **Interior view,** black and white contrast
shapes the building
→ | **Wall,** Beola stone

Wellness Area of Matteo Cambi

Parma

The challenge of this design consisted of linking together the different functions of the
bathroom, bedroom, dressing room and wellness area in an open design covering 82 m².
A particular highlight of the concept is the integrated bathtub made of Beola stone. The
other materials were also carefully chosen for their effects – black smoked oak parquet
floors coupled with Brazilian Beola stone are contrasted with white Cervaiola marble. All
furniture pieces were especially designed by Pagini+DiMauro and theatrically as well as
effectively staged with the spotlight illumination concept.

PROJECT FACTS **Address:** Parma, Italy. **Builder-owner:** Matteo Cambi. **Completion:** 10.2005. **Area:** 22 m² (bathroom), 60 m² (wellness area).

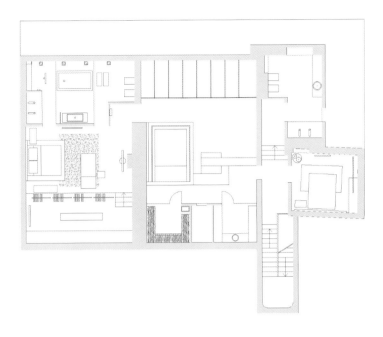

←←| **Interior view**, washbasin
↑ | **Floor plan**
←↙↓| **Interior view**, bathroom

↑ | **Bathing zone** with copper tub
↗ | **Spa,** hot stone made of marble
→ | **Lead bathroom** with vital illumination

Dornbracht Elemental Spa
Ritual Bathroom

Ritual architecture is the result of the interaction of space and acts of cleansing, in which human beings are at the center of the architectural design. The bath becomes the interface between the user and his/her rituals. Emphasizing the archaic, the products of the Elemental Spa concept were deliberately designed for this ritual architecture purpose and constitute a contemporary interpretation of elementary water springs. These water springs have a clear, cubical shape distinguished by the mouthpiece with the crystalline-like inner shape. The soft water discharge accentuates the feeling of standing near a natural spring.

PROJECT FACTS

Builder-owner: Dornbracht. **Area:** 100 m² (with patio). **Exhibition:** ISH 2007 Frankfurt / Main. **Product concept and design:** Sieger Design. **Ritual architecture:** Mike Meiré.

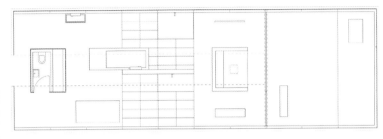

←← | **Detail**, corten steel
← | **Elemental spa**, hidden mirror
↑ | **Floor plan**
↙ | **Watering place**, archaic shower
↓ | **Ritual**, place for washing feet

Terrazzo Werkstatt
Regensburg
Michael Dorrer

↑→ | **Monolithic masterpiece,** inside surface of polish grinding, outside of brushed concrete

Badeei

Ulm

Following the tracks of the old terrazzo masters, Michael Dorrer's "Badeei" was crafted as an artisan masterpiece. In addition to the well-known terrazzo floors, the material was also previously used to create bathtubs whose shape was adjusted to that of the human body. Since the tub is increasingly used as a monolithic instrument in bathroom design of today, the "Badeei" is therefore a combination of tradition and modernity. In addition to the choice of the egg shape (goose, chicken or sparrow), another challenge was posed by the construction method. Finally, a method exactly opposite to slipforming, in which the egg permanently rotates around its longitudinal axis through the interior and exterior skin of the shell, produced the desired result.

PROJECT FACTS
Address: Bundesfachschule für Betonwerker, Ulm, Germany. **Completion:** 10.2005. **Length:** 2.17 m. **Max. diameter:** 1.36 m. **Surface:** 7 m². **Wall thickness:** 3.5 cm. **Weight:** approx. 600 kg.

4°

Joseph Caspari Architect

Espace PAYOT

Paris

↑ | **Main room,** wall: white marble from Carrare and Cardoso grey stone revetments
↗ | **Footbridge** crossing the pool to the "chamber of mirrors"
→ | **Bar** from a block of Cardoso grey stone

In the spirit of classic bathing parlors, the only elements present are water, stone and light. The purity of the used lines and materials contributes to the relaxing effect, while their decorative qualities stem from the unique rhythm of the spaces and their monolithic spirit. The ubiquitous presence of the minerals lends a timeless character to the whole setting. Inside the walls of a building dating back to the beginning of the last century, the ensemble is situated on two levels. The ground floor contains the reception area, dressing rooms and services, while the underground level features a swimming pool, Jacuzzi, hammams, saunas, a gymnasium as well as cubicles for health and beauty treatments.

PROJECT FACTS
Address: 62 rue Pierre Charron, 75008 Paris, France. **Builder-owner:** PAYOT. **Construction time:**
8 months. **Completion:** 10.2006. **Construction sum:** € 4,500,000. **Main usable floor area:** 1,700 m².
Project management: Gilbert Jacomy.

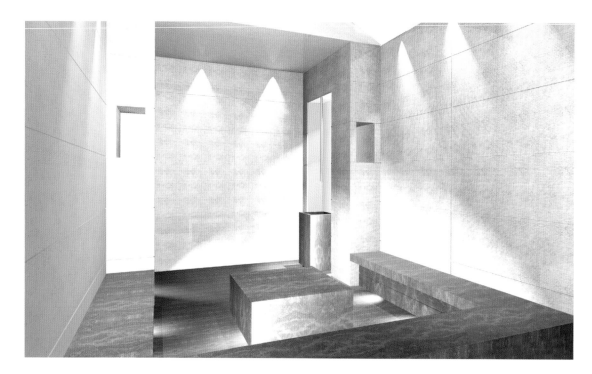

↑ | **Hammam Femme,** drawing
↓ | **Section,** underground level

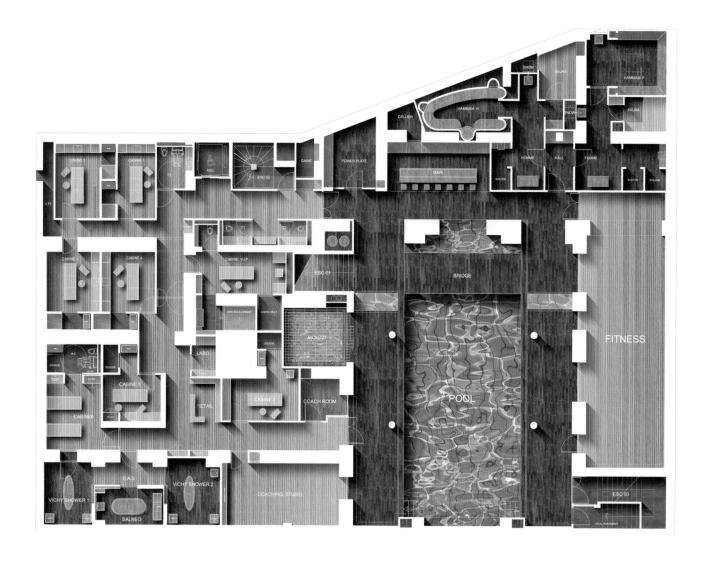

← | **Swimming pool,** view to the bar
↙ | **Hammam,** wash basin
↓ | **Hammam,** marble block

Dirkjan Broekhuizen
Interieurarchitect BNI

↖ I **Bathtub,** Starck edition Hoesch
↑ I **Washbasin,** Marike/Jeurissen
↗ I **Window sill,** Silestone
→ I **Floor plan**
→→I **Floor tiles,** Mosa/Schans Veenendaal

Private Bathroom
Epse

The residents of a bungalow in Epse, who were retiring after many years spent abroad, asked Dirkjan Broekhuizen to redecorate their bathroom in a "spacious, simple in a practical way and warm" style. The walls are dominated by mauve, since bed sheets and towels were already present in this favorite color that is also found in other rooms of the residence. In addition to specially designed closets and towel holders, the bathroom features a large dual washstand and a free-standing tub, as well as a large easily accessible shower with two fixed shower heads and a handheld shower handle. The wall, which is covered in 60x60 cm tiles, includes a storage rack, while a glass panel with the word "WET" has taken the place of the former connecting door to the hallway.

Address: Epse, Gelderland, The Netherlands. **Builder-owner:** private. **Area:** 8.8 m² (bathroom).

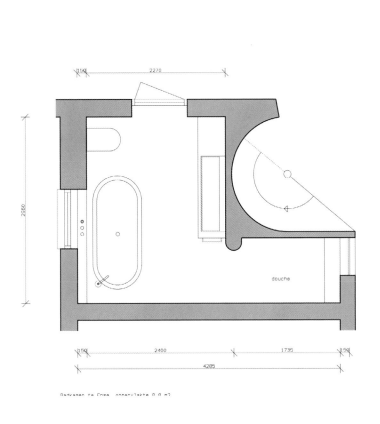

gmp – Architekten
von Gerkan, Marg
und Partner

↑ | **Liquidrom,** underneath the raw
concrete dome shell
→ | **Cloakroom**

Liquidrom
Berlin

The Liquidrom is the third event hall within the Tempodrom with a water basin of 13 meters in diameter, vaulted by a domed concrete shell featuring a top light in its zenith. Light and sound define the atmosphere of the Liquidrom. Up to 50 visitors lying in lukewarm salt water can enjoy an impressive concert experience with light installations, underwater loudspeakers and four sound columns. In addition to the circular saltwater basin, the Liquidrom also consists of several saunas, steam baths, a hot water open-air basin, which is called "Onsen" in the Japanese tradition, as well as a bar and a restaurant.

PROJECT FACTS

Address: Möckernstrasse 10, 10963 Berlin, Germany. **Builder-owner:** New Tempodrom Foundation. **Completion:** 03.2002. **Gross area:** 1,360 m². **Design:** Meinhard von Gerkan. **Partner:** Hubert Nienhoff. **Project management:** Stephan Schütz. **Project team:** Wilfried Schoo, Matthias Wiegelmann, Ulrike Bruttloff, Nicolas Pomränke, Patrick Pfleiderer, Johannes Erdmann.

↑ | **Exterior,** plunge bath enclosed with
timber walls
↓ | **Section and floor plan**

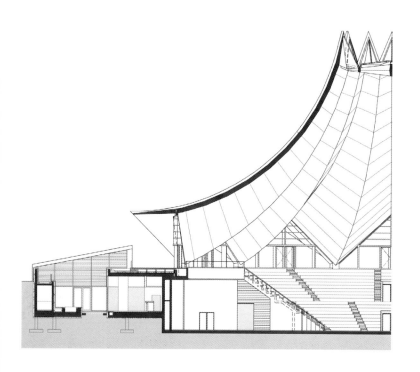

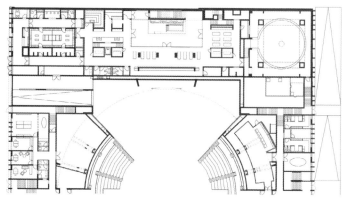

← | Changing room
↓ | View towards the atrium

Michael Schmidt
code.2.design

↑↗ | **Bathroom furniture,** graphical form in
contrast with organic hollows
→ | **Sketch**

Shape Collection
Bathroom furniture

The Shape Collection by Michael Schmidt combines oak with the mineral composite
Cristalplant into a minimalist piece of bathroom furniture that balances hard and soft
shapes. The elliptically shaped sink of the vanity is elegantly incorporated into the rectangular basic shape of the horizontal block. The drawers of the vanity unit close silently,
while the mirror can be illuminated by the touch of a finger. The shape of the sink was
designed to resemble a rock hollowed out by a mountain brook.

Client: Falper, Via Veneto 7–9, 40064 Ozzano Emilia – Bologna, Italy.

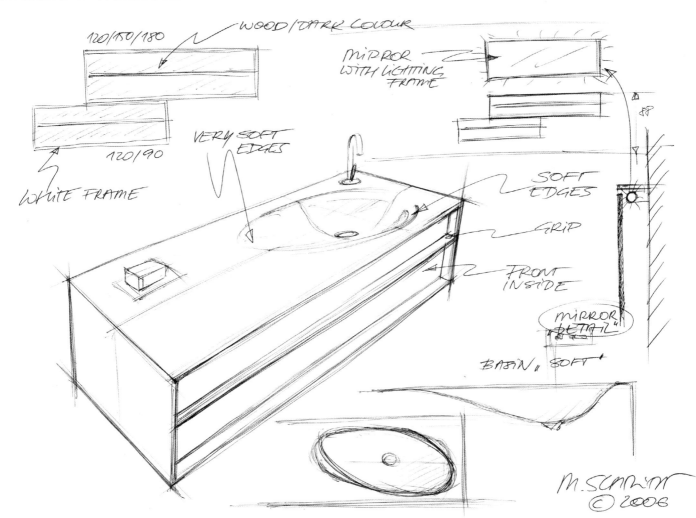

Mario Botta

↑ | **Exterior view,** detail of the "leaves" made of titan zinc and glass

↓ | **Exterior view, Turkish bath, interior view from "Water World"**

Tschuggen Bergoase
Arosa

Arosa offers the extraordinary geographic configuration of a natural basin surrounded by mountains. It is a place with a constant contrast between man and nature, emphasized by the powerful landscape in which the ancestral fight between man and mountain is evident.

The site of the newly built Bergoase consists of a free space and park at the foot of the rear mountain next to the great hotel. The architect's concept consists of building without building, asserting the presence of the new through the added parts (artificial trees as metaphor of the nature) and combining the huge area with the functional program. The cover of the lower spaces is designed as a stage marked by geometric planted shapes that rouse the visitor's curiosity.

PROJECT FACTS
Address: Tschuggen Grand Hotel, 7050 Arosa, Switzerland. **Builder-owner:** Tschuggen Grand Hotel AG.
Completion: 2006. **Area:** 5,300 m². **Volume:** 27,000 m³.

↑ | **Interior view,** bridge between the spa and
the hotel

↓ | **Spa area,** relaxation benches in "Water World"

↑ | **Night shot,** nine "trees of light"
↓ | **Section**

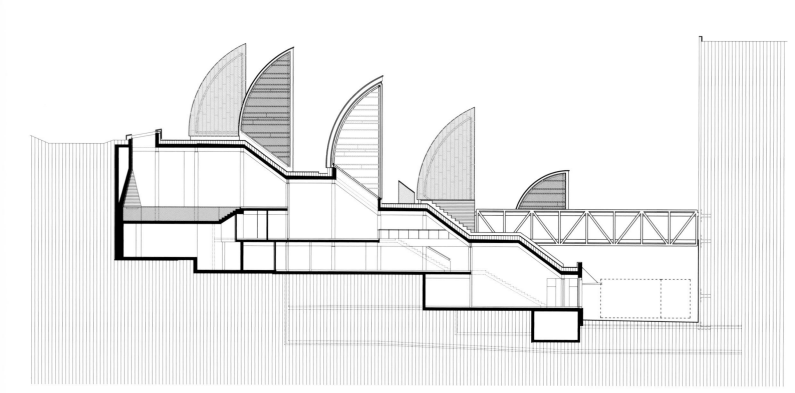

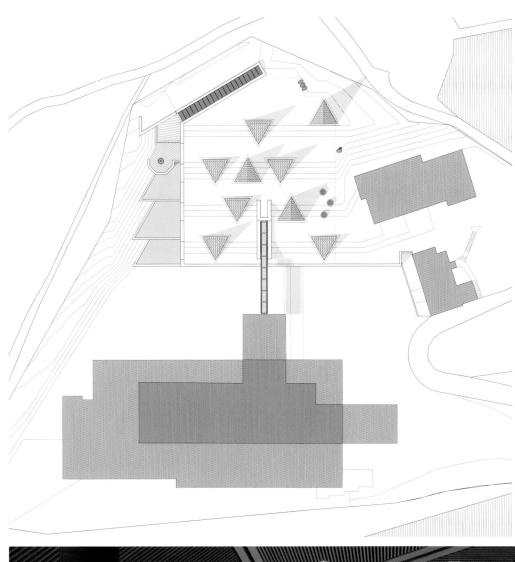

← | **Site plan**
↓ | **"Water World"**, roof consists of triangular modular panels made of Canadian maple

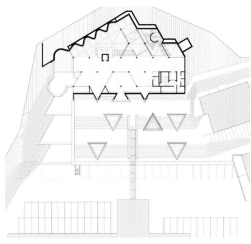

←←| **Detail of the curved wall in "Water World"**
← | **Sketch** by Mario Botta
↑ | **Third floor plan**
↓ | **Interior view,** pool area

Finkeldey + Uetrecht
nexus product design

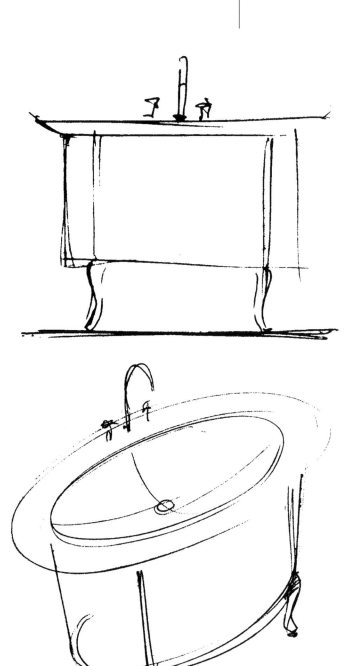

↖ | **Sketch**
↑ | **Interior view,** bathroom furniture Diva Series
↓ | **Washstand,** detail

Burg Diva
Bathroom furniture

The shapes of this extravagant line of bathroom furniture pay homage to the classical, sometimes opulent design of furniture and its manufacturing by highly skilled artisans. The materials used consist of rosewood and nutwood in combination with highly polished lacquer. By interacting with various styles, tastes and materials, Diva is intended to also set the stage for experiencing great emotions while bathing.

Address: burgbad AG, Bad Fredeburg, Germany. Year: 2006.

Crepain Binst Architecture
(Luc Binst)

↑ | **Exterior view,** black cemented façade with
two pictograms in front of the possible children's
rooms
→ | **Bathroom** sunk into the floor

Lofthouse
Humbeek

The architect wanted to organise life around him in his home, so that it would become
an instrument, a kind of lab consisting of various spheres and functions, which minimal
interruptions or partitions would allow to flirt with one another. Being unable to generate
the powerful effect that was sought with a room-based dwelling in which enjoyment of
home invariably occurs in a fragmented setting, transitions were eliminated and everything was organised as one large entity – a single tableau in which everything interrelates
in a new scale context. The bathroom is sunk into the floor above the ground-floor toilet.
From the shower, one has a good view of the living area, kitchen and projection wall for
TV, video and DVD.

PROJECT FACTS

Address: Kerkstraat 53, 1851 Humbeek, Belgium. **Construction time:** 2003–2004. **Construction costs:** € 500,000. **Total floor area:** 500 m². **Interior designer:** Luc Binst, Tom de Meester. **General contractor:** Janssens bvba.

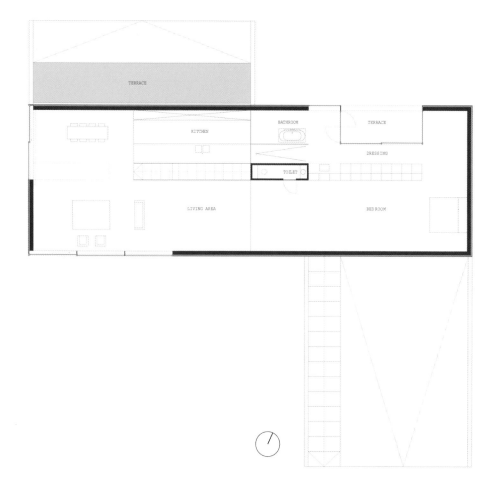

↑ | **Interior view,** lounge atmosphere
← | **Floor plan**

← | **Bathroom,** poured synthetic resin floor in bright blue
↙ | **Shower** (1.1 x 3.6 meters) with a laternal drainage strip
↓ | **Detail,** 10-meter long black dressing closet

Yves Collet

↑ | **Exterior view,** spa in the vineyards

The French Vinotherapie®
Spa Caudalie

Bordeaux

Located in the heart of the renowned Chateau Smith Haute Lafitte vineyards in Bordeaux, this spa was elected second best destination spa in the world by Travel + Leisure magazine in 2007. The refined atmosphere of the treatment rooms, the clever blend of wood, stone and the building itself, which is reminiscent of old tobacco kilns, were all designed for one purpose – to combine the virtues of naturally hot spring water drawn from 1,771 feet under the earth – rich in minerals and oligo-minerals – with the most recent scientific discoveries regarding the benefits of the vine and its grape.

PROJECT FACTS

Address: Chemin de Smith Haute Lafitte, 33650 Bordeaux-Martillac, France. **Builder-owner:** Caudalie.
Opening: 1999.

↑ | **Sun-bathing terrace**
← | **Interior view,** pool
↓ | **Floor plan**

↑→ | **Interior view,** bathroom furniture

Private Bathroom
Hamburg

During the redesign of the living area that previously served as a bedroom, the existing floorboards and windows were preserved. The renovation created a large mounted piece of bathroom furniture that incorporates all essential functions and with enough space for the plumbing in its pedestal. Within the new living quarters, the bathroom constitutes a functional element as well as an independent piece of furniture.

PROJECT FACTS
Address: Hamburg-Harvestehude, Germany. **Builder-owner:** Familie Lang-Bognar. **Completion:** 05.2002. **Area:** 200 m².

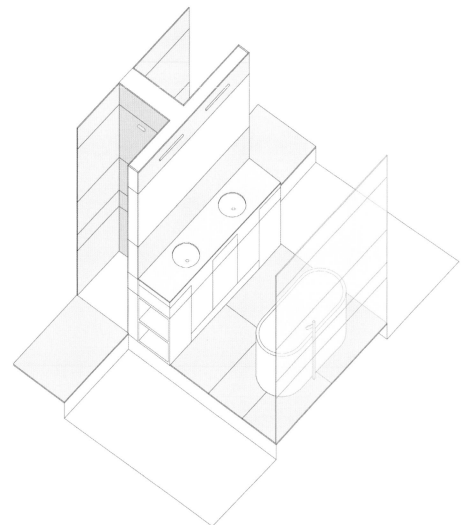

← | **Isometry**
↓ | **Bathroom furniture** on existent wooden floor
→ | **Hide-out,** shower behind the mirror

Markus Wespi
Jérôme de Meuron
Architekten BSA

Residential Home

Brione sopra Minusio

The new building is located in a densely developed high-class residential area above Locarno with a view of the city, the lake and mountains. The design is the understated reaction to an everyday topic – building in the chaos of urban development. This is why it does not include any of the attributes of a classical house. It consists only of two simply shaped cubes that are offset to each other and push out of the mountain. They are fragmented, seeming to belong to the landscape rather than to the urban setting, jérôre of a wall than a house, and cannot be assigned to a specific architectural era.

Habitable interior rooms were created by the process of excavation. Two homogenous large openings that can be closed with wooden gates provide residents with access from and a view of the outdoors. Additional light is provided by inner courtyards. The water of the swimming pool built into the cube on the valley side is combined with the lake.

↑ | **Exterior view,** swimming pool made of exposed concrete
→ | **Interior view,** natural stone wall

PROJECT FACTS **Address:** 6645 Brione sopra Minusio, Switzerland. **Construction time:** approx. 18 month. **Completion:** 2005 (house), 2006 (outdoor facilities). **Area:** 533 m². **Living space:** 95 m². **Construction management:** Guscetti Arch. Dipl., Minusio.

↖ | **Sketches**
← | **Section**

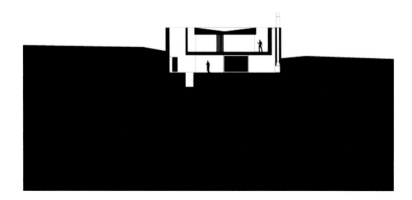

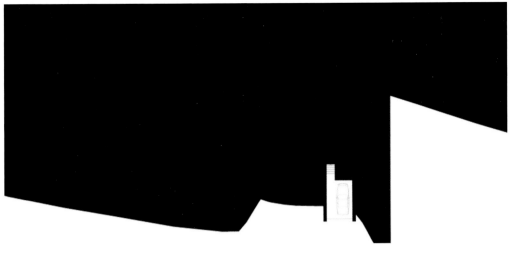

← | **Section**
↓ | **Exterior view,** swimming pool

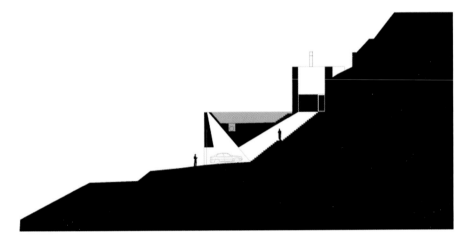

Jeff Etelamaki
Design Studio

↑ | **Point of purchase,** back lit acrylic wall
→ | **Ceiling mural**

Bliss Spa Soho

New York

During the update of Bliss' original spa and retail premises, the space was reconfigured to create more product display areas and improve client traffic flow. Original signature design elements were maintained as a gesture to the spas' important role in the history and success of the company. An existing circular ceiling mural was preserved and the new fixtures, architectural details and graphic elements were designed in relation to this prominent feature. Freestanding curved fixtures emulate the form of the mural while creating a dynamic spatial flow. A laminated acrylic "feather wall" used in the original design was also re-created and incorporated into the flagship store location.

Address: 568 Broadway, 2nd floor, New York, NY 10003, USA. **Builder-owner:** Blissworld, LLC. **Completion:** 2006. **Main usable floor area:** 10,000 ft².

←←| **Fixtures from the Royal Promotion
Group,** www.royalpromo.com
↖ | **Sketch**
↑ | **Floor plan**
↓ | **Treatment area,** upper floor, waiting room

Nieberg Architect

↑ I **Washstand,** concrete

→ I **Skylight**

Residential Home
Lehrte

The building consists of a single family home that underwent a redensification of the existing structures. The result is an interesting combination of weightiness and lightness that is also manifested in the bathroom, which has been created as a freestanding element in the center of the surrounding space. Fitted closets in the recesses of the access areas on both sides function as dressing areas. The light entering from the glass façades is transferred on both sides through glass walls or doors into the bathroom. A four m² skylight additionally illuminates the enclosed middle area containing the washstand and the opposite WC/bidet. The residents are given the impression of standing under the open sky without being seen. The materials of the bathroom, alternating massive fair faced concrete walls with the lightness of satined glass walls, are based on the overall concept of weightiness and lightness. In addition to the underfloor heating, the dimmable open light strips with their orange light create a comfortable mood.

PROJECT FACTS
Address: Westpreussenstrasse, 31275 Lehrte, Germany. **Builder-owner:** Detlef Klose. **Planning and construction time:** 10.2000–05.2004. **Gross floor area:** 397 m². **Lighting:** Axel Nieberg.

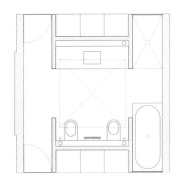

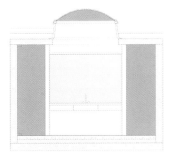

←← | **Bathtub and Shower**
← | **Exterior view**
↑ | **Floor plan and section**
↙ | **WC/bidet**
↓ | **Bathtub**, mood lighting

↑ | **Pontoon** (800 m²) with a modular "Ringhaus" construction
→ | **Whirlpool** made of red cedar

Spa Wolfsburg
Wolfsburg

Since early June 2005, a swimming pool has been afloat in the port basin of the Autostadt between the parking lot and power plant of the VW factory premises. Connected only via a small pier to the spa area and thus the solid ground, the floating pool is a fresh water outdoor pool offering a clean body of water within the harbor allowing users to experience swimming in the canal and the port basin. It follows the tradition of the so-called "bathing ships", of which fifteen private Spree swimming pools existed in Berlin alone at the turn of the last century. These swimming pools either consisted of a partitioned section of water within the Spree river or contained pools filled with fresh water.

PROJECT FACTS
Address: Port basin of the VW Autostadt, Wolfsburg, Germany. **Builder-owner:** Autostadt GmbH. **Completion:** 06.2005. **Construction time:** 61 days (buildings), 35 days (swimming pool). **Size:** approx. 30,000 m². **Pontoon:** 800 m². **Net area:** 130 m². **Gross volume:** 577 m³.

← ← | **Floating tanks**
← | **Swimming pool,** transportation
↓ | **Relaxation area,** benches of concrete with
integrated heating wire

↑ | **Aerial view**, swimming pool (40x9 meters)
← | **Floor plan**

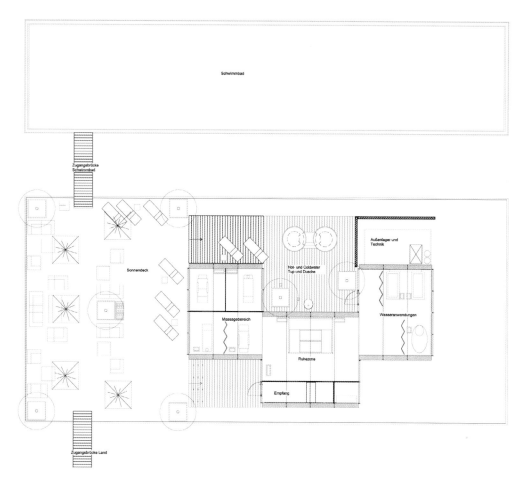

Schwimmbad

Zugangsbrücke
Schwimmbad

Sonnendeck

Massagebereich

Hot- und Coldwater
Tup und Dusche

Außenlager und
Technik

Wasseranwendungen

Ruhezone

Empfang

Zugangsbrücke Land

← | **"Ringhaus" construction,** glass fronts
facing East and West
↓ | **Spa building** made of charcoal-colored
fibrous concrete and three-layered Oregon pine
boards

Ron Arad

↑ | **Interior view,** bulbous, rounded shapes

Hotel Puerta America, Level 7
Madrid

A curved, continuous wall, painted white in some rooms and bright red in others, acts as a central divider separating the different uses of the space. Arad creates a circuit in which guests gradually discover each of the spaces. Bit by bit they first discover the entryway, then the bed, then the bathroom, the sink, and the toilet. There are no limits; it is like a dream world. In the bathroom, the spaces are made independent of each other by a wall divider, and despite their continuity, their logical independence is not forsaken. The shower and toilet have stainless steel ceilings. Blended, both materials create an extremely modern space with a touch of high technology. On the opposite side is a huge swath of glass, which as a casing of the toilet not only provides a distorted reflection of the guest, but also visually enlarges the space.

PROJECT FACTS

Address: Avenida de América 41, 28002 Madrid, Spain. **Builder-owner:** Grupo Urvasco. **Completion:** 2005. **Area:** 1,200 m². **Project team:** Ron Arad (principal designer), Geoff Crowther, Egon Hansen, Marta Granda, Djordje Stojanovic. **Lighting:** Isometrix.

↑ | **Continuous walls,** red in some rooms, white in others

↓ | **Floor plan and section**

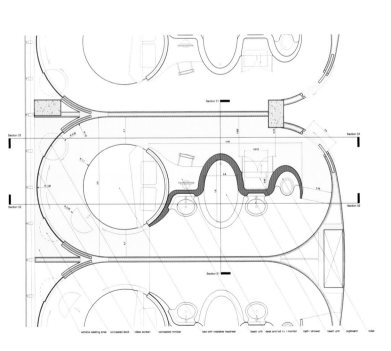

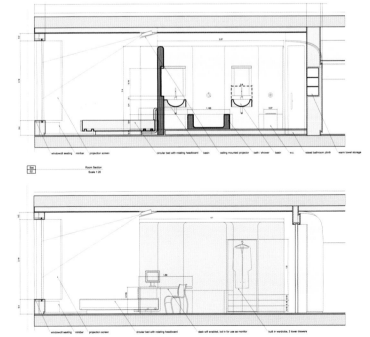

↑ | **Exterior view,** façade without roof overhang   → | **Interior view,** shower

House K
Gmund am Tegernsee

Construction guidelines in the area around Lake Tegernsee are quite restrictive. How then should the qualities of a traditional Bavarian cultural landscape, thoroughly worthy of preservation be treated while also giving justice to the demand for a renovation that takes advantage of contemporary design resources? The result was a typologically simple house that conforms to all guidelines governing roof shape and pitch (15–25 degrees), materials and others. The house is embedded in the steep slope of the parcel and incorporates the marvellous views onto Lake Tegernsee. The structure is distinguished by its façades, the roof made of split larch shingles that are spread across the surfaces like a snakeskin, and the lack of a roof overhang. The house is also characterized by its economical and painstaking details.

PROJECT FACTS
Address: Kramerweg 13, 83703 Gmund am Tegernsee, Germany. **Planning and construction time:** 2002–2005. **Area:** approx. 1,500 m². **Living space:** 229 m². **Project team:** Dipl. Ing. Daniela Spuhler, Dipl. Ing. Helmut Schmid, Dipl. Ing. Stefan Krippl.

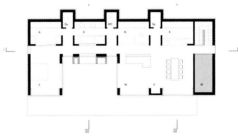

←← | **Bathroom**
← | **Façade,** larch shingles
↑ | **Floor plan**
↓ | **View from the bathtub**

↑ | **Blue Spa,** roof terrace

Blue Spa
Hotel Bayerischer Hof, Munich

The Blue Spa extends across three floors, covering a total area of 1,200 m². Located on the fifth floor, the materials used for the beauty center and changing rooms create a comfortable "cave-like" atmosphere. Above this area extends the roof garden swimming pool, laid out with mosaic stones in a bright blue color dotted randomly with silver and black, which was the inspiration for the new name of the wellness area. The glass roof above the pool can be opened within seconds during fair weather. The newly added seventh floor houses the Blue Spa Bar & Lounge as well as a winter garden that can be used in a multifunctional way due to its folding sliding wall, both featuring a view of the Frauenkirche (Church of our Lady).

PROJECT FACTS

Address: Hotel Bayerischer Hof, Promenadeplatz 2–6, 80333 Munich, Germany. **Builder-owner:** Hotel Bayerischer Hof, Gebrüder Volchardt KG, Innegrit Volchardt. **Opening:** 05.2005. **Construction costs:** € 7 million. **Area Blue Spa:** 1,200 m². **Project supervision and construction engineering:** Architekturbüro Augustin und Partner, Munich. **Design of gym equipment:** Ralf Moeller, Los Angeles.

↑ | **Pool** (14.5 x 6 meters), opened roof

↓ | **Pool,** closed roof

↑ | **Roof terrace,** view of the Frauenkirche and the town hall
↓ | **Floor plan**

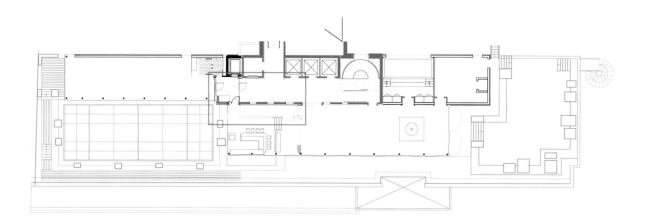

← | **Blue Spa,** entrance sauna
↓ | **Relaxation room,** floor and wall of dark-grey granite

Wieki Somers

↑ | **Bathboat,** vehicle on dry land

↓ | **Sketch**

Bathboat
Limited Edition

A water vehicle on dry land sparks the imagination – it comes to mind that the concepts of floating on the water or bathing in the water have many similarities, as both are a pleasurable diversions. They evoke such similar feelings and deal with such similar elements that they are combined in one installation in the Bathboat. By turning a small boat inside out it becomes a bathtub, while bathtub legs are reminiscent of the wooden frame on which the boat usually rests when it is docked. The Bathboat is actually a vehicle on dry land in which the mind can drift away, or drift home after a full day with shiploads of information. It will wash away the dust of the city.

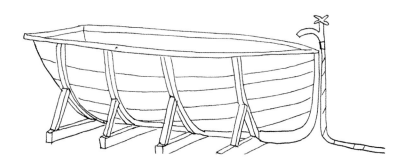

PROJECT FACTS

Height: 1,950 mm. **Width:** 850 mm (incl. legs 1,000 mm). **Diameter:** 600 mm. **Weight:** max. 50 kg. **Material:** red cedar and oak wood, epoxy, dd-lacquer. **Colours:** grey-white, wood. **Distribution:** Gallery Kreo.

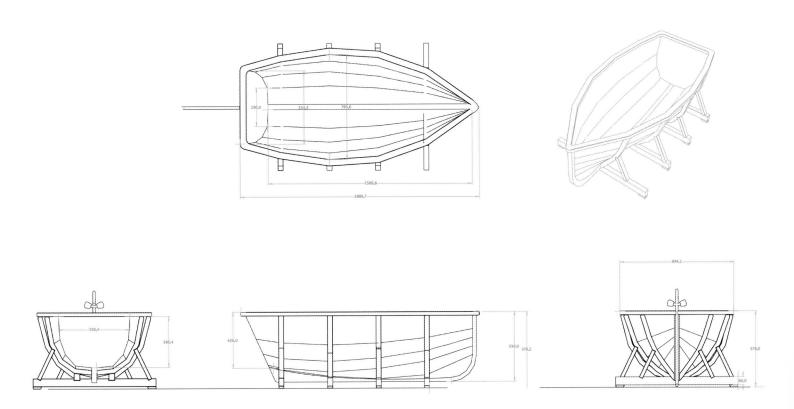

↑ | **Sketches**
↓ ↘ | **Bathboat,** made of red cedar and oak wood

↑ | **Bathroom,** detail
↗ | **Bathroom,** mosaic stripes fall by Bisazza
↗↗ | **Bathroom,** backlight mirror, custom-made by
F1 Arredamenti, accessories by Vola
→ | **Floor plan**

Bisazza Showroom
Berlin

Fabio Novembre, who already designed several mosaics series for Bisazza, created this showroom using the Stripes Fall series. With their clear shapes and warm fall colors, the small gemstones create a comfortable atmosphere. Simultaneously, the clear geometric stripes that evolve into a circle from a straight line create a concentric eddy that attracts the eye of the beholder similar to a pebble that is thrown into a pool of water.

PROJECT FACTS

Address: Bisazza Berlin Showroom, Kantstrasse 150, Berlin, Germany. **Builder-owner:** Bisazza S.P.A. **Opening:** 11.2003. **Area:** 250 m². **Design team:** Carlo Formisano, Lorenzo De Nicola, Giuseppina Flor, Ramon Karges. **Contractor:** Löhn Hochbau GmbH. **Local architect:** Arch. Carlo Lorenzo Ferrante – ION industrial design.

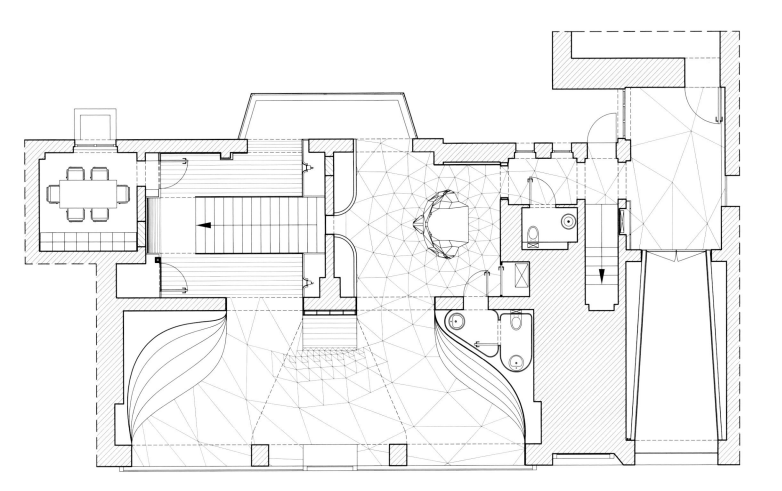

D E SIGNSTUDIO
REGINA
DAHMEN-INGENHOVEN

↑ | **Exterior view,** façade
↓ | **Section**

→ | **Interior view,** shower

Health Center Lanserhof

Lans near Innsbruck

Harmonic shapes, materials in their natural state, a pleasant play of colors, smooth floors, transparency and careful attention to minute details – the architecture of 1,500 m² futuristic medical, therapy and beauty center is distinguished by its uniqueness and consistency. A special challenge of this extension was the combination of old and new. The result was particularly harmonious, natural, simple, beautiful and authentic. The cliché-free architecture and the design express the positive attitude towards life and the energy that were released here. A gentle world was created featuring rounded edges, soft colors, shapes and materials, inviting visitors to relax and regain their strength. Light plays an important role in this world of well-being and energy. The light is never direct, glaring or distressing. Regina Dahmen-Ingenhoven describes the concept of recesses with an almost sacral atmosphere in which the light sources can often only be vaguely discerned as "healing light."

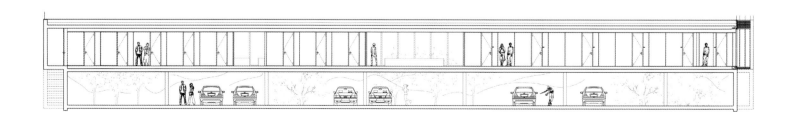

PROJECT FACTS

Address: Kochholzweg 153, 6072 Lans near Innsbruck, Austria. **Builder-owner:** Health Center Lanserhof, Lans. **Completion:** 2005. **Construction sum:** € 3 million. **Gross volume:** 5,000 m³. **Lighting:** Tropp Lighting Design, Feldafing. **Project partner:** Jan Görgemanns.

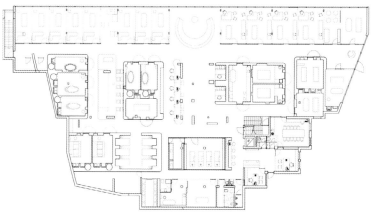

←← | **Translucent, 50-meter long wall** with a mountain panorama view
↙↙ | **Detail,** Liquid Energy
↑ | **Floor plan**
← | **Kneipp area,** Bisazza mosaic
↓ | **Softroom**

↑ | **Smart Spa Studio**, reception
→ | **Treatment room**, eggplant-colored

Yi Spa
Berlin

The Yi presents a holistic spiritually balanced lifestyle concept – understated elegance, natural elements like slate stone, mother-of-pearl and dark wood are contrasted with colored glass, exotic plants and delicate fragrances. The idea was to allow all these elements to interact distinctively, while certain design features, like the tone-in-tone gravel between big stone slabs that imposes a path through a riverbed in Chiang Mai, exemplify the correlation between interior design and tradition. The Yi Spa integrates Asian culture into a modern realistic ambiance.

PROJECT FACTS **Address:** Monbijouplatz 3a, 10178 Berlin, Germany. **Builder-owner:** xix Gesellschaft mbH, Marco Thiele & Stephan Gustavus. **Completion:** 2006. **Main usable floor area:** 120 m². **Gross volume, interior:** 420 m³.

←← | **White room,** "room bracket"
← | **Interior view,** eggplant-colored room
↑ | **Detail,** "room bracket"
↓ | **Interior view,** black room

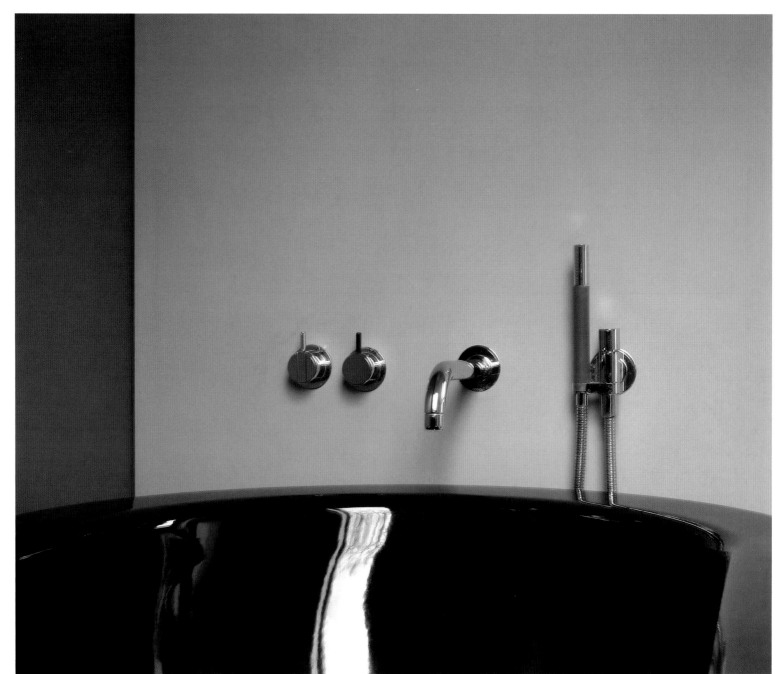

↑ | **Bathtub faucets**
→ | **Washstand**

Restructured Villa

Hanover

The aura of the landmarked villa dating back to the 1920s is derived from its handcrafted red brick walls. Only in the roof area new openings for additional illumination were created. The added gallery level enables open living spaces. A translucent blue glass wall separates the living area and the bathroom. The preservation regulations allowed only limited openings in the roof, which is why the disproportionate illumination of the bathroom compared to the other areas, had to be balanced. Specifically developed for this project, the blue color of the glass wall filters the light and transmits it to the living area. The bathroom floor is covered in smoothed black slate. The walls are merely plastered and waterproofed. Functional areas are defined by the two-meter high wall panes, while the elevated bathtub is a suspended element that adds lightness to the bathroom. The extensive mirror on the wall behind the washstand expands the room size and allows the background view of the tree tops of the adjacent forest.

Address: Herderstrasse, 30625 Hanover, Germany. **Builder-owner:** collective ownership. **Planning and construction time:** 1998–2000. **Gross floor area:** 550 m². **Lighting:** Axel Nieberg.

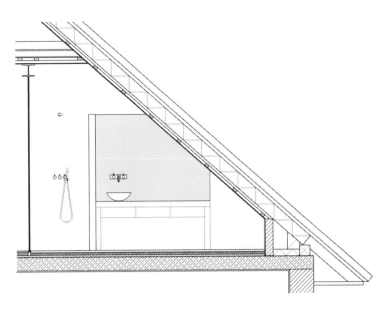

←← | **Interior view,** bathtub
← | **Shower**
↑ | **Section**
↙ | **WC alcove**
↓ | **Entrance** to the bathroom

Jean Nouvel

↑ | **Interior view,** sliding panels with photographies of Araki
→ | **Panels** allowing guests to organize the room with photographies of Alain Fleischer

Hotel Puerta America, Level 12
Madrid

Two names in particular leave their signatures on this work. They are those of photographers Nobuyoshi Araki and Alain Fleischer. Based on the original idea of using pleasure as the theme of this floor, Nouvel decided to display the work of these photographers that plays with atmospheric images of the human body and nature. Executive suites have a system of sliding panels with floor and ceiling rails that allow guests to organize the room space to their liking. Using this most unusual feature, the guests themselves become architects, reorganizing the space for themselves. Do you want a big bathroom, or perhaps an extra-large living room? These panels make it all possible.

PROJECT FACTS
Address: Avenida de América 41, 28002 Madrid, Spain. **Builder-owner:** Hoteles Silken. **Construction time:** 2004–2005. **Completion:** 07.2005.

← | **Floor-to-ceiling photographies**
by Nobuyoshi Araki and Alain Fleischer
↓ | **Level 13,** swimming pool and roof

Julie Mathias

Indulgent Bathing

Concepts for future bathrooms

↑ | **Dream bathroom,** Jungle
→ | **Bathroom design,** Pleated

"Indulgent bathing" is a series of design projects resulting from one year of research at the Helen Hamlyn Research Center in partnership with the bathroom manufacturer Ideal Standard. The aim was to create a less cool and neutral bathing environment that is rather inspired by storytelling and emotional experiences. The strongest statements of each user, which were mainly related to fear, smell, nostalgia or passion, were explored by the designer. The discovery of a treasure of strong feelings translated into the users' own bathroom concept, resulting in six concepts each related to an individual user. These became narratives that directly fed into a series of design concepts that collectively propose a sensual and refreshingly different design language for the bathroom. Each user had a very different approach to bathing, for some it was a hiding place, while others saw it as a meeting point.

PROJECT FACTS **Address:** London, United Kingdom. **Client:** Ideal Standard. **Year:** 2005.

145

←← | **Bathroom design,** Tree
← | **Knot,** toilet
↓ | **Dream bathroom,** Drop

↑ | **Exterior view,** Zen garden
→ | **View of the lake,** pool made of exposed concrete

Private Swimming Pool

Vico Morcote

As part of the overall development concept, three swimming pools were set out in a single line to highlight the clear outlines of the modern residential units. For this particular house, the pool was positioned between the house and an old mill. The pool is made of exposed concrete to give justice to the natural color of the lake in the distance. Below the mill, the formerly destroyed 200-year old millpond was fixed, equipped with a filtering system and stocked with koi fish. With loving attention to detail, a setting was created that resembles a Zen garden, providing visitors with a sense of inner calm upon entering. Everything is balanced and as it should be with earth, water and sky combined into a single unit.

Address: 6921 Vico Morcote, Switzerland. Builder-owner: private. Completion: 2004. Project architect: Martin Wagner, Carona.

↑ | **View from inside,** Zen garden
↓ | **Floor plan**

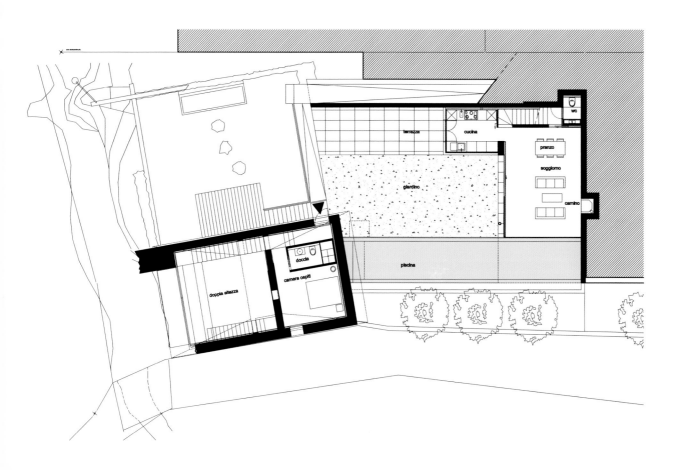

← | **Millpond** with koi fish
↓ | **Neighbors:** living and water

Jaime Hayon ArtQuitect

↑ | **Interior view,** Elegant Series
↓ | **Detail,** hangers

AQ Hayon Collection
Bathroom furniture

The collection offers a variety of accessories for customization, a multi-purpose glazed cabinet and a series of glass and ceramic containers. It is a revival of the elegant bathrooms of former years, when bathrooms represented the social status of the home or a restaurant. It is a return to the past with an eye on the future and aims to recover the distinction of beautiful objects in our time. This project renews our commitment to bathroom culture and gives the bathroom back the elegance of earlier times, without sacrificing modernity in the shapes or the functional nature of the pieces. These new bathrooms have changed their status and do not have to hide anymore.

Address: ArtQuitect, Dolors Granés 79, 08440 Cardedeu (Barcelona), Spain. **Year:** 2005.

↑ | **AQ Hayon Collection,** Volume 2
↓ | **Interior view**

↑ | **Illustration**

←← | **Interior view,** Colorful Series
← | **Mirror,** detail
↓ | **Sketchbook**

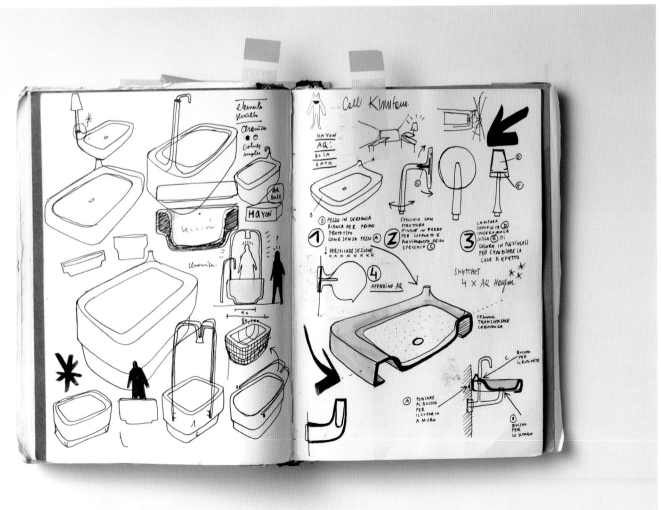

YES-architecture

↑ | **Exterior view** from the West
↓ | **Detail,** outdoor pool

Residential Home

Graz

The single-family home was built on a steep, strongly southward sloping hill. Due to the steepness of the slope, it was necessary to build the construction as stacked terraces. The house was planned to properly present an art collection and to allow the merger of private and business interests. The result is a steel-plate covered widely extending structure whose unique dimensions only become fully apparent when ascending to the entrance. The English basement, featuring a home cinema, wellness rooms and basement, is mainly shifted to the side, leaving the space under the house empty. The whole structure resembles the glamorous architecture of modernity in California and could serve as the setting for a James Bond movie, right up to the urinal that is freely placed in front of the glassed view of the city.

PROJECT FACTS

Address: Graz, Austria. **Builder-owner:** private. **Completion:** 05.2007. **Construction costs:** € 1 million. **Net floor area:** 340 m². **Area:** 846 m².

←↑ | **Interior view**, children's bathroom
↓ | **Floor plan**

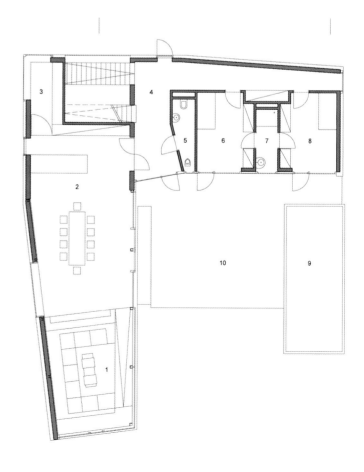

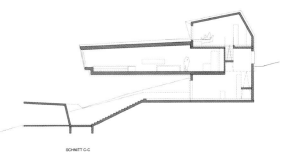

SCHNITT C-C

←↓ | **Interior view,** bathroom
↑ | **Section**

Dirkjan Broekhuizen
Interieurarchitect BNI

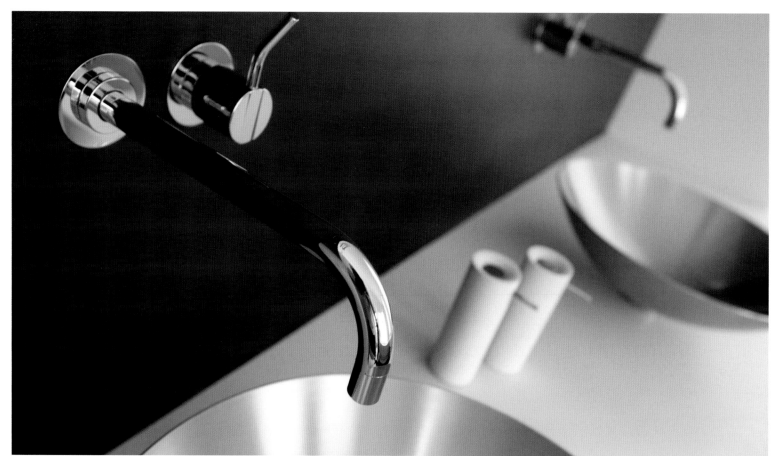

↑ | **Faucets,** Vola

Private Bathroom

Velp

It was the wish of the residents of the villa at the edge of the forest near the city of Velp to be able to look into their garden from the bathroom. Broekhuizen, working in close cooperation with the owner, allowed the quiet atmosphere and the wish for simplicity to guide him. The 12.5 m² bathroom is dominated by the expansive glass front. The eye catcher is the u-shaped installation made of Silestone, into which the bathtub has been integrated. The towel holders and fitted closets were designed especially for this bathroom. To allow the view of nature, the bathtub is positioned on a wooden pedestal that almost seems to make it float. Only the walls of the shower are covered in tiles. The second bathroom of the residence for the children sized 6 m², was accentuated by the color green which is reminiscent of the green of nature.

PROJECT FACTS

Address: Velp, Gelderland, The Netherlands. **Builder-owner:** private. **Area:** 12.5 m² (bathroom), 6 m² (children's bathroom).

↑ | **Interior view,** view of the forest

↓ | **Bathtub,** Casandra by Villeroy & Boch

↑ | **Washbasin,** stainless steel, by Alape
↓ | **Floor plan**

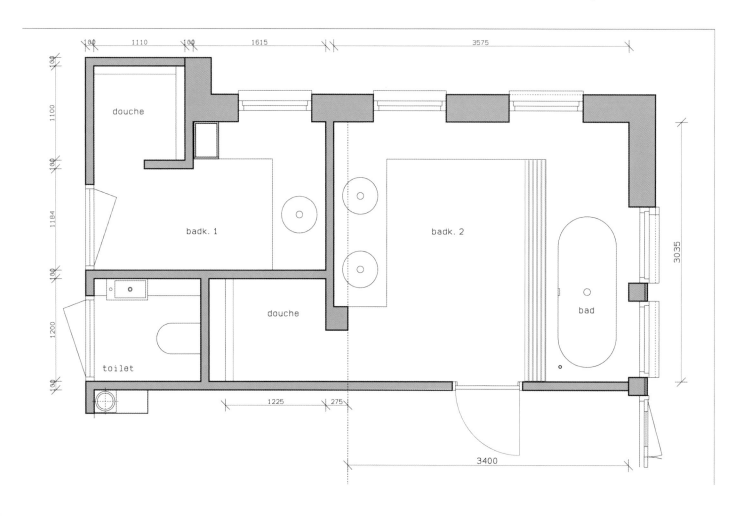

← | **Exterior view**, pond
↓ | **Shower**, Raindance by Hans Grohe

↑ | **Washbasin,** yellow marble hand-made in Bali
→ | **Floor and wall covering,** Corten by Tau
Cerámica

Private Bathroom
Geleen

At first the bathroom had a normal ceiling height of 2.4 meters with a multitude of edges. After studying the room, the decision was made to take out the ceiling and raise the wall up to four meters. This way, a ceiling ranging from four meters on one side to 90 cm on the other could be created. The relatively big bathroom allowed the addition of a large walk-in shower of 180 cm in width. The owners decided to give the room a dark and warm look. The combination of dark brown colors and stainless steel was approved. They were especially fond of the Corton Rust tiles to which a mosaic was matched.

PROJECT FACTS

Address: Geleen near Maastricht, The Netherlands. **Builder-owner:** private. **Completion:** 08.2006. **Interior designer:** Gatto V.O.F., Geleen. **Master builder:** Gatto V.O.F., Geleen.

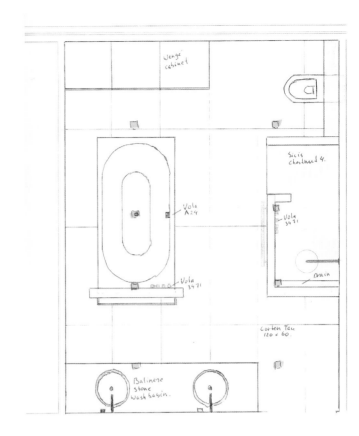

←← | **Detail faucets,** Vola brushed steel
← | **Shower head,** Fantini
↑ | **Floor plan**
↓ | **Bathtub Sphinx** surrounded by Wenge veneered panels with lighting

↑ | **Bathroom,** view of the lake
→ | **Detail,** washbasin with window instead of a mirror

House See-Eck
Berlin

During the restructuring of the landmarked residential home, its main floor was turned around. The principal rooms, including the large bathroom, now no longer face the street but the lake. The built-in additions with their prolific interiors behind low-key exteriors add another corresponding layer to the existing structures. The ongoing theme, which is also applied to the three bathroom areas of the residence, consists of framing that delineates boundaries and structures as well as connections.

PROJECT FACTS **Address:** Lietzenseeufer 10, Berlin-Charlottenburg, Germany. **Builder-owner:** private. **Planning and construction time:** 04.2002–01.2003. **Construction costs:** € 300,000. **Living space:** 350 m². **Design team:** Nils Stelter, Sabine Kühnast. **Statics:** Eisenloffel+Sattler Ingenieure. **Building construction:** Andreas Adam. **Joinery:** Frank Spitzer.

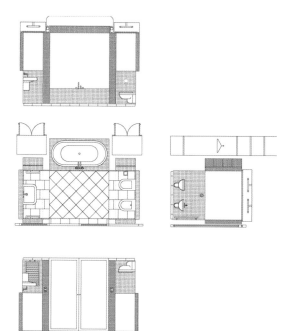

↑↓ | **Plans and floor plan**
← | **Built-in units:** left wardrobe, right toilet

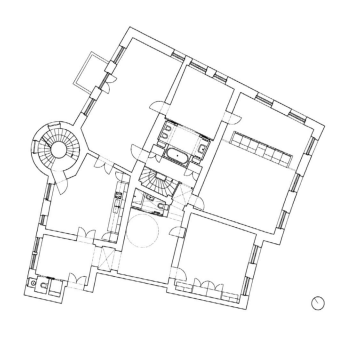

← | **Bathroom** in alcove
↓ | **Bathtub** with large mirror

↑ | **Suite 5,** bathtub design by Marcel Wanders
(Bisazza)
↓ | **Floor plan**

→ | **Suite 6,** Bisazza mosaic wall

Lute Suites
Amsterdam

Lute Suites is the first "urban" project of its kind in the world. A row of exquisitely beautiful, 18th century cottages, all featuring views of the Amstel River, have been converted
into seven suites fitted out with every imaginable comfort while the interiors are utterly
unique in every detail. The contribution of the illustrious design labels Boffi, Bisazza and
Moooi was instrumental in realizing this ambitious concept. The appeal of the Lute Suites
is that the guests enjoy complete freedom of movement combined with truly homely surroundings. Each suite has its own front door and comprises a living room, a separate bathroom and a separate bedroom. In the living room, a kitchenette and a wine rack provide
homelike comforts, while the flat screen TV/DVD invites guests to take off their shoes
and wind down at the end of the day.

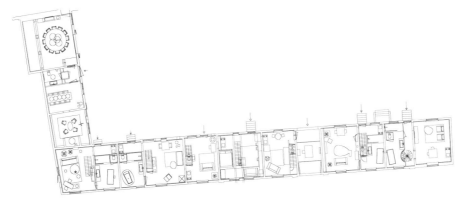

PROJECT FACTS

Address: Amsteldijk Zuid 54–58, 1184 VD Ouderkerk aan de Amstel, The Netherlands. **Builder-owner:** Lute Suites (Peter Lute, Marieke Lute and Marcel Wanders). **Completion:** 01.2005. **Concept:** Marcel Wanders Studio. **Design:** Marcel Wanders Studio (Marcel Wanders, Karin Krautgartner). **Project team:** Marcel Wanders, Karin Krautgartner, Rebecca Wijsbeek.

↑ | **Suite 3,** zinc design fixtures
← | **Suite 1,** bathtub Gobi (Boffi)

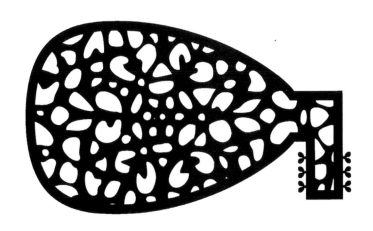

↑ | **Lute Suites logo**
← | **Suite 5,** soap bath by Marcel Wanders
(Bisazza)
↓ | **Suite 5,** wall with printed tiles (Art on tiles)

↖ | **Pool,** concrete shell, teak wood millwork
→ | **Bar,** flanked from changing rooms

G Spa & Lounge
The Hotel Gansevoort, New York

An unparalleled dual space opened in Manhattan's Meatpacking District. Located within one of New York City's hippest hotels—The Hotel Gansevoort— the new venue is an innovative leisure space. The "grotto" level of the hotel was renovated and transformed into the G Spa & Lounge. The first spa / private club hybrid of its kind, G Spa & Lounge was designed to provide both a soothing and relaxing environment for spa-goers by day and a sleek private club by night. The innovative dual use of space positions the project in a class of its own.

PROJECT FACTS

Address: The Hotel Gansevoort, 18 9th Avenue, New York, NY 10014, USA. **Builder-owner:** William and Michael Achenbaum. **Completion:** 02.2006. **Size:** 4,300 ft². **Project team:** Bob Henry (architect), Nicole Migeon (manager), Harris Levy, Gary Yen, Rebecca Wu (design team).

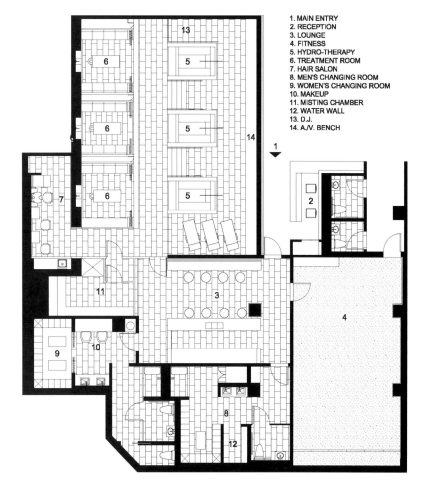

1. MAIN ENTRY
2. RECEPTION
3. LOUNGE
4. FITNESS
5. HYDRO-THERAPY
6. TREATMENT ROOM
7. HAIR SALON
8. MEN'S CHANGING ROOM
9. WOMEN'S CHANGING ROOM
10. MAKEUP
11. MISTING CHAMBER
12. WATER WALL
13. D.J.
14. A./V. BENCH

↑ | **Racing stripe,** 40 feet long
← | **Floor plan**

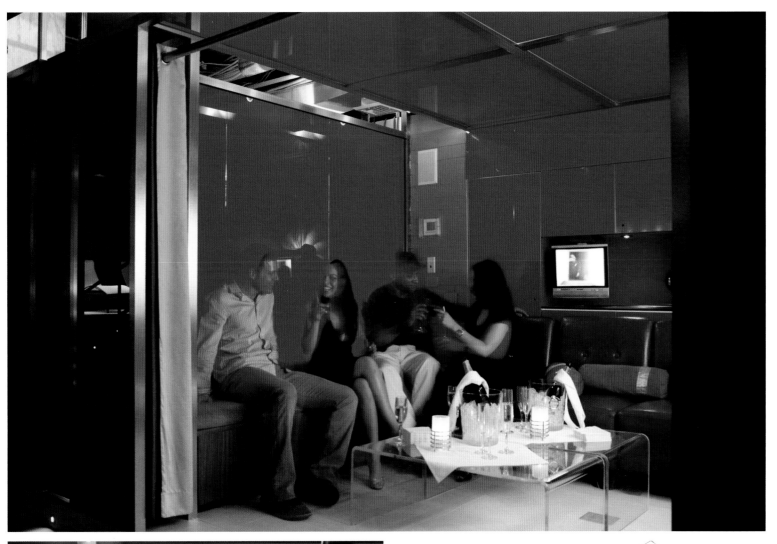

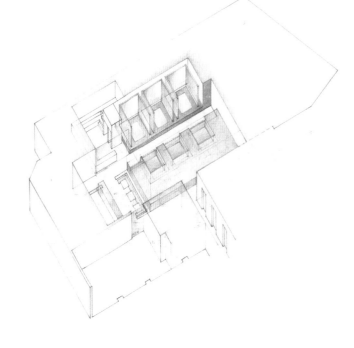

↑↑ | Lounge area
↑ | Illustration
← | Hydrotherapy pool

GRAFT Architekten
Lars Krückeberg
Wolfram Putz
Thomas Willemeit

↑ | **Hotel room,** bathtub and bed
→ | **Coexistence:** bed and basin

Hotel Q
Berlin

At the location of the Knesebeckstrasse, GRAFT created a hotel landscape that changes the classic spatial concept through the topographical folding option of its different elements. The tectonic logic of element construction is distorted and blends into hybrid zones with double functionalities. The inclined area is at the same time a separating wall as well as a usable furniture item, while the elevated floor acts as a circulation surface or a space, emerging from beneath the surface of the house. The inhabitants become participants in this landscape, changing their interaction with architecture and furniture, like walking up the walls to sit on top of a celebrating crowd, or by sinking into tubs that resemble hot springs in the floor in the middle of the room.

PROJECT FACTS
Address: Knesebeckstrasse 67, 10623 Berlin, Germany. **Operator:** Loock Hotels. **Completion:** 03.2004.
Construction costs: € 9 million. **Floor area:** 3,200 m². **Gross volume:** 12,000 m³. **Project development and owner:** Wanzl & Co Bauträgergesellschaft KG. **Project architect:** Wolfgang Grenz. **Project team:** Johannes Jakubeit, Michael Rapp, Sascha Ganske.

↑ | **Sketches**
← | **Beach feeling:** spa area with sand
↓ | **Section**

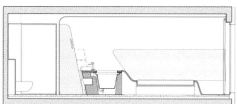

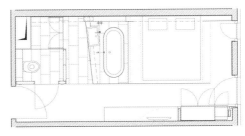

← | **Interior view,** room
↑ | **Section**
↓ | **Spa area,** shower with wooden benches

Jacques Garcia

↑ | **Interior view,** relaxation room
→ | **Swimming pool,** detail

La Réserve Genève Hotel & Spa
Geneva

In the heart of a beautifully landscaped park of ten acres on the shores of Lake Geneva, the hotel has regained the majesty of former years. Elegant yet relaxed, homely yet fashionable, a new spirit emanates over one of Geneva's most mythical hotels. It offers 2,000 m² dedicated to the art of well-being, a unique environment to renew body and mind. La Réserve Spa offers a full range of personalized treatments targeting three key areas: healthy age management, nutritional advice, and deep relaxation. The overall approach is specifically adapted to each guest's individual needs following an in-depth assessment. The hotel contains 17 private treatment rooms, indoor pool, fitness center, hair salon, sauna, and steam bath.

PROJECT FACTS
Address: 301 route de Lausanne, 1293 Bellevue, Geneva, Switzerland. **Area:** 2,000 m².

185

↑← | **Interior view,** swimming pool

← | **Underwater music,** heated 16-meter
indoor pool
↙↓ | **Interiors,** reminiscent of an African lodge

100°

↑ | **Spa,** concealed under a still water mirror
→ | **Rendering,** exterior view

Mahn Spa Hotel

Puerto Vallarta

Visitors are submerged in a parallel universe – a physical and emotional sanctuary of well-being. As a recurrent component, water is treated like a source of energy, materializing itself in abundance in the atmosphere in the form of ice, fluid, steam or as elusive reflections representing various climates. The hotel appears like a pebble invaded by plants or like a peaceful island standing on the quiet lake of the public spaces. It features a biblical entrance – visitors walk on water and go through a liquid curtain pouring alongside its majestic stairs. Located inside the pebble, the bedrooms are protected from the world by the lake, while the spa lies concealed under a still mirror of water.

Address: Puerto Vallarta, Mexico. **Area:** 7,500 m² (total), 2,500 m² (rooms), 3,000 m² (public area), 2,000 m² (technical area). **Construction sum:** $ 50 million.

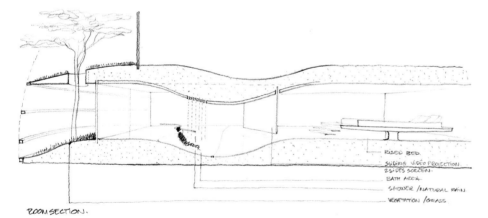

ROOM SECTION.

RISED BED.
SLIDING VIDEO PROJECTION
2 SIDES SCREEN.
BATH AREA.
SHOWER / NATURAL RAIN
VEGETATION / GRASS

↑ | **Massaud Design,** Axor for Hans Grohe
← | **Sketch**

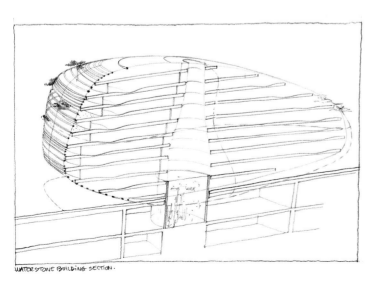

WATERSTONE BUILDING SECTION.

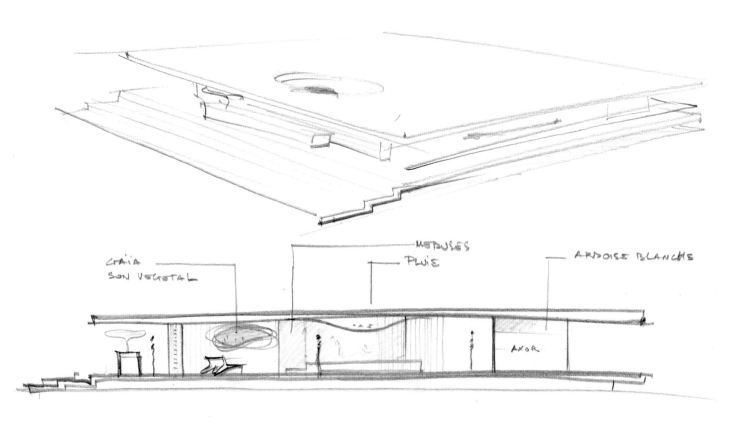

CRAIA
SON VEGETAL

MEDUSES
PLUIE

ARDOISE BLANCHE

AXOR

↑ | **Sketch**
↓ | **Massaud Design,** Waterdream

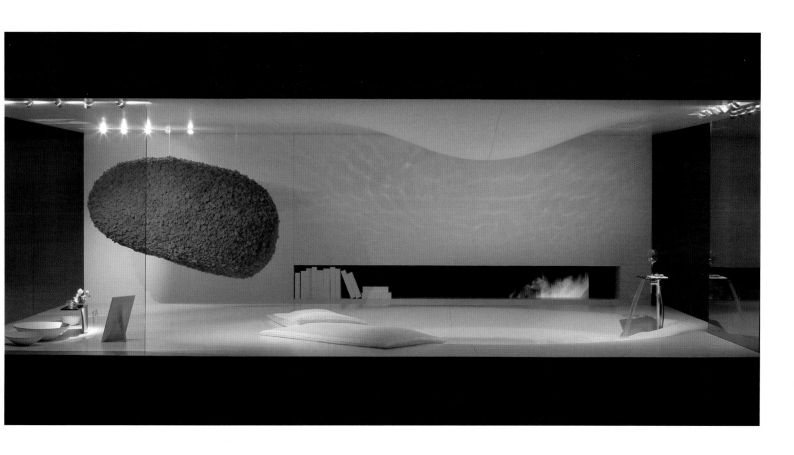

↑ | **Jacuzzi,** Relaxo with spillway by Riviera Pool
→ | **Sauna,** heater by EOS, control unit by OSF

Penthouse
Private Bathing Area

Lungo Lago

The restructuring of the former Hotel Excelsior at the Lungo Lago into an apartment building enabled the creation of a private bathing and fitness area in the penthouse. Completely noise insulated from the rest of the house, it offers a perfect relaxation zone. The available space was cleverly used so that a Jacuzzi, sauna and steam bath could be implemented. Dark walls made of individually fitted sandblasted slate sheets eclipse the room and contrast with the bright Jacuzzi. Oiled teakwood was used for the floors and the ceiling, and overall a bathing area was created whose harmonious design offers an excellent indoor environment coupled with superb functionality.

PROJECT FACTS
Address: former Hotel Excelsior at the Lungo Lago, Italy. **Builder-owner:** private. **Area:** 25 m² (bathroom).

195

↑ | **Interior view,** walls made of sandblasted slate sheets
← | **Jacuzzi,** lighting by Hydroair

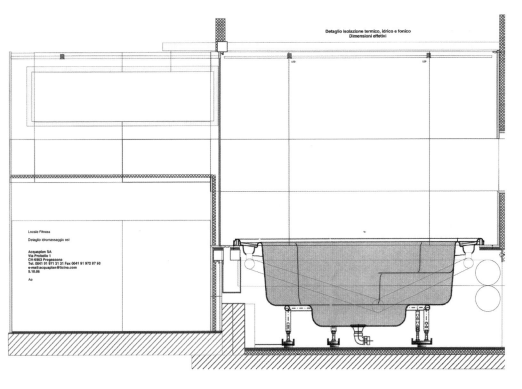

← | **Section**
↓ | **Wall and ceiling shower** with rain and waterfall functions, integrated steam bath

Ushi Tamborriello
Innenarchitektur &
Szenenbild

Fitness and Wellness Park

Baden

↑ | Meditation bathroom
↗ | Fitness bathroom
→ | Steam bath

The fitness park is located in the new section of the Trafo complex. The light-flooded open structure of the ground floor with a view of the surrounding greenery, the Trafo, as well as the Brown Boveri Platz, offers optimal training conditions. The large-size course swimming pool is the architectural core of the basement floor. The 95 m²-sized pool is only perceived as a quiet surface of water at the rear of the room, which it completely occupies. Wooden platforms of varying heights are positioned in front of the body of water, inviting guests to linger. Next to it, the meditation pool can be accessed via a stairway leading into the mysteriously shimmering water. The dry meditation room does not intensively stimulate the senses, instead focusing on the essential – tranquility. The steam bath is a room installation enabling new spatial perspectives with its perceived tapered construction combined with light and steam effects.

PROJECT FACTS

Address: Brown Boveri Platz 1, 5400 Baden, Switzerland. **Builder-owner:** Genossenschaft Migros Aare.
Opening: 11.2005. **Construction sum:** approx. CHF 6.5 million. **Area:** 740 m². **Project management:** S+B
Baumanagement AG, Olten. **Project development:** Roger Bernet, rob. d-sign, Aarau.

Yves Collet

↑↗ | **Interior view,** relaxation area
↗↗ | **Exterior view hotel,** architect:
Frank O. Gehry
→ | **Treatment rooms**

Spa Vinotherapie®
Caudalie Marques de Riscal

Elciego

In the Spanish wine-growing region of Rioja Alavesa, where the grapevines stretch all the way to the horizon, a luxury hotel was opened in 2006 in the vicinity of a 140-year old winery. Frank O. Gehry designed a luxury hotel for the Spanish winery "Marques de Riscal" in the wine-growing region of Rioja. The building complex consists of several intermingled cubes. A bold roof construction towers over the whole complex, providing it with an unusual visual highlight, featuring an almost freely suspended titanium outer layer. The spa located inside was designed by Yves Collet in line with the Caudalie philosophy.

Address: Calle Torrea 1, 01340 Elciego, Spain. **Builder-owner:** Caudalie. **Opening:** 2006. **Floor area:** 1,500 m². **Architect (hotel):** Frank O. Gehry. **Other involved designers:** Philippe Lamy (painter), Bénédicte de Lescure (designer).

↖ | **Shower**
↑ | **Illuminated stone wall,** LBM fiber
technology
→ | **Pendant lamp** by Moooi

Hotel de France

Spa in the Empire Wing, Jersey

The Hotel de France on the green Channel Island of Jersey is one of the few privately run hotels of its size in Europe. As the foundation pit of the spa had to be literally carved into the mountain, while the historic parts of the building were to be combined gently with the new wing of the building, stone was chosen as the predominant material. The spa is equipped with a 15-meter long glass façade that can be lowered into the ground. On fair weather days it is completely lowered, connecting the pool space to the outdoor area. The RGB System, which provides diffused and glare-free illumination to the ceiling areas, allows the adjustment of the lighting according to the daylight situation or the desired room ambiance, for example bright yellow-orange in the morning and dark blue at night.

PROJECT FACTS

Address: St Saviour's Road, St Helier, JE1 7XP Jersey, United Kingdom. **Builder-owner:** Hotel de France.
Commencement of extension: 2002. **Architects:** Haertwig Grassl Architekten. **Lighting design:** Licht 01.
Project team: Katja Winkelmann, Robert von Sichart.

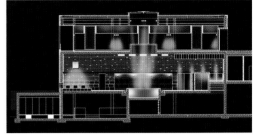

← | **Color change,** RGB System Luxmate,
Zumtobel
↑ | **Lighting,** Schwarzplan
↓ | **Interior view,** pool by night

Fabio Novembre

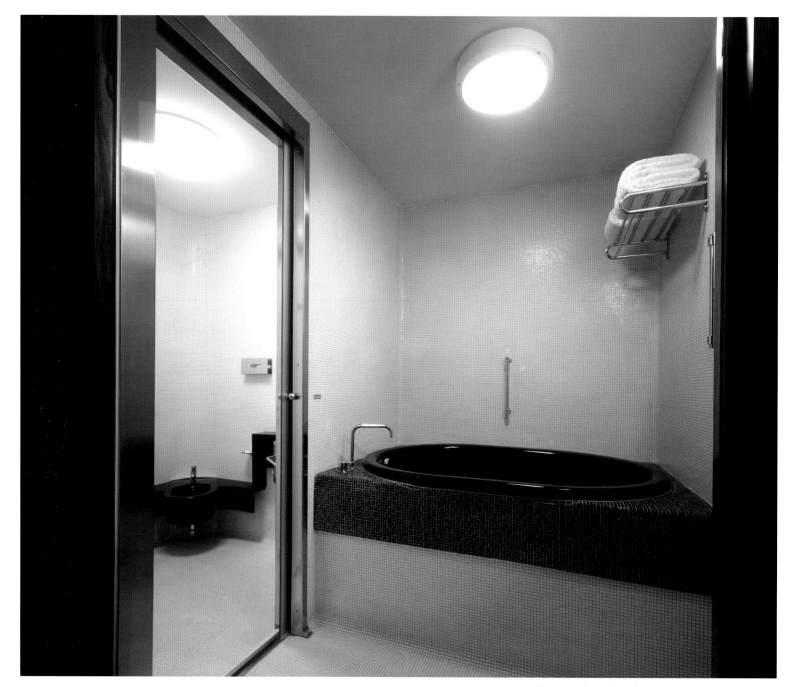

↑ | **Interior view,** bathroom, mosaic Vetricolor
by Bisazza
→ | **Bathroom**

UNA Hotel Vittoria

Florence

The hotel is more than a design hotel. The structure and the layout of the spaces revolutionize the concept of hospitality. The concept promotes the idea of the hotel as a "theatre of life", a place where guests not only sleep but also live and work in a regenerating and energizing atmosphere. A continuous flow of emotions permeates the entire hotel, which combines historic and artistic Florentine hospitality with the latest design and technology in a captivating, ironic and breathtaking harmony of shapes and colors. The internal spaces have been divided into many independent but connected functional areas alive with warm shades and materials such as mosaics, leather and printed lamé.

PROJECT FACTS

Address: UNA Hotel Vittoria, Via Pisana 59, Florence, Italy. **Builder-owner:** UNA Hotels and Resorts. **Opening:** 06.2003. **Area:** 4,000 m². **Contractor:** Tino Sana. **Design team:** Carlo Formisano, Lorenzo De Nicola, Giuseppina Flor, Ramon Karges.

←←| **Shower,** mosaic Vetricolor by Bisazza
←| **Interior view,** wall covering leather by
Cuoium, laminated print by Locatelli
↓| **Floor plan**

↑ | **Interior view,** pool
↓ | **Details,** Turkish sauna, outdoor pools, piazza

→ | **Detail,** outdoor pool

Therme Meran

Merano

The Therme Meran represents a link between mountains and water. Nature is incorporated into the building and constitutes its dominating element – the materials of stone, wood and glass preserve their tactile and emotional characteristics. "High touch" denotes the development of architecture from the "nature" of elements involving untreated, natural surfaces that can be experienced with the hands, feet and eyes. The distinguishing element of the bath hall is the large light installation consisting of multi-colored discs and spheres that appear to be freely suspended in space as they slowly turn. Light is reflected in many shades of color, moving along the walls and across the surface of the water. When the different colors are superimposed they result in new hues – an effect similar to the sunset. The room acts as a dynamic continuum of light and color that frees the perception of all types of concreteness.

PROJECT FACTS

Address: Therme Meran, Thermenplatz 9, 39012 Merano, Italy. **Builder-owner:** Meraner Kurbad AG.
Opening: 12.2005. **Water surface:** 2,000 m². **Architecture competition, concept, building input, details:**
Baumann Zillich Architekten, Berlin. **Implementation planning architecture/interior/lighting:** Matteo
Thun & Partners, Milan. **Team:** R. C. Precoma, M. Catoir, G. Bastiani, P. Scifo, S. Ronchi, S. Fumagalli,
C. Toscano, L. Colombo.

↑ | **Interior view,** treatment room 1
← | **Interior view,** treatment room 2

← | **Exterior view**, glass cube by night
↓ | **Night shot**, indoor pool

↑ | **Hotel room,** washbasin
→ | **Detail,** mirror facets

Hotel Puerta America, Level 4
Madrid

A different architect/interior designer of international standing was commissioned to create each floor, turning the hotel into a vertical juxtaposition of contemporary architecture. In the rooms of the fourth floor, a long meandering sheet of stainless steel becomes the main organizing element of the room. Moving along the back wall, it starts as a desk, turns into a headrest then a seat. It "crashes" into the glass division wall and mutates into a bathtub and finally the shower. The folded glass wall that divides the bedroom from the bathroom has also become another product of distortional forces. The two pieces of furniture seem to have crashed perpendicular into a single pane, transforming it into a prism that breaks light and presents views in ever-changing oscillating configurations.

PROJECT FACTS
Address: Avenida de América 41, 28002 Madrid, Spain. **Builder-owner:** Hoteles Silken. **Construction time:** 2004–2005. **Completion:** 07.2005. **Main usable floor area:** 1,260 m². **Project management:** Ferrovial.

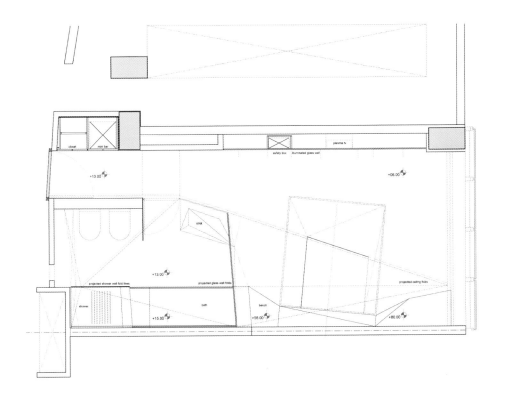

←← | **Interior view**
← | **Floor plan**
↓ | **Hotel room,** open bathroom

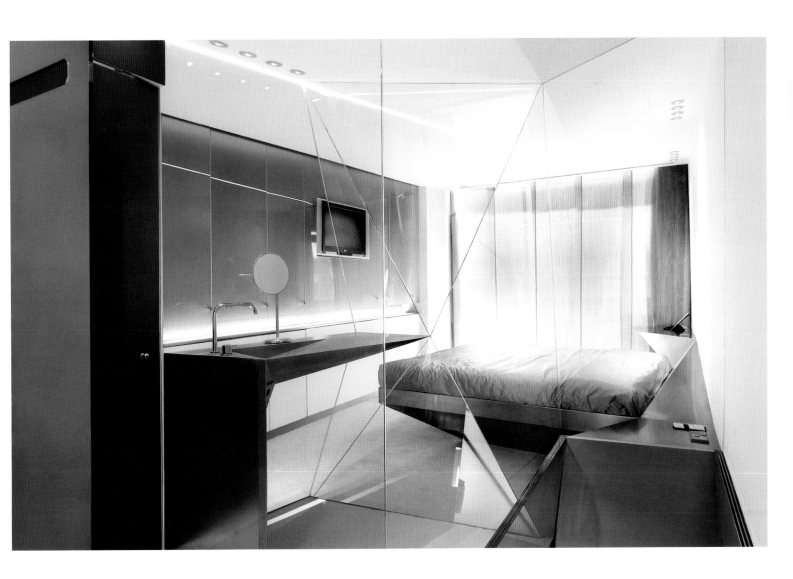

G. Hakan Kulahci

↑ | **Spa,** relaxation area
→ | **Exterior view,** outdoor pool

The Dome Spa
Kempinski Hotel The Dome, Belek

Located in an area of natural beauty also known as the Turkish Riviera, the Kempinski Hotel The Dome lies directly near the beach. It offers various relaxation options for its guests look in. The Dome Spa embraces one of Turkey's largest spa and Thalasso facilities, including extra large outdoor pools and an outdoor Jacuzzi. Spread over 3,600 m², The Dome Spa offers facial, body and Thalasso treatments as well as a variety of saunas, a heated indoor swimming pool, a heated seawater pool and a genuine Ottoman Hamam, all laid out in exclusive, refined settings. In 28 carefully appointed and equipped treatment rooms and sections, guests can enjoy a true oasis of relaxation.

PROJECT FACTS

Address: Kempinski Hotel The Dome Belek-Antalya, Uckumtepesi Mevkii, 07500 Belek, Turkey.
Builder-owner: Akkanat Holding. **Completion:** 2005. **Area:** 3,600 m². **Project management:** Ahu Tecim, Ayhan Koken.

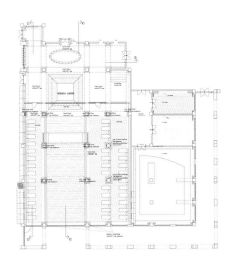

←← | **Interior view,** pool
← | **Lighting,** detail
↑ | **Floor plan**
↓ | **Interior view,** changing lighting

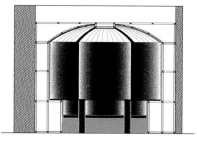

A-A KESİT

↑ | **Interior view,** changing lighting
← | **Floor plan and section,** Thalasso Steam
Room

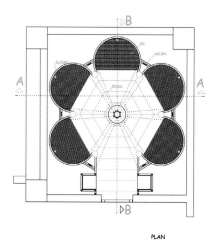

PLAN

B-B KESİT

←↓ | **Interior views,** pool

↑ | **Interior view,** view of the shower
↗ | **Detail,** washbasin, toilet and bathtub
→ | **Floor plan**

Apartment
Berlin

The primary elements used in this project are light and shadow, as well as opacity and transparency. These immaterial elements allow the space to adjust to the passing of time throughout the day or the year. The space becomes a dynamic composition loaded with potential energy. The experience is very subtle, one has to be in a receptive state of mind, while the spatial experience has to be powerful enough to break the boundaries of reason, to submerge the senses and touch the spirit.

Address: Berlin, Germany. **Construction time:** 8 months. **Completion:** 2001. **Main usable floor area:** 121 m². **Design:** Helmut Jahn & Yorgo Lykouria.

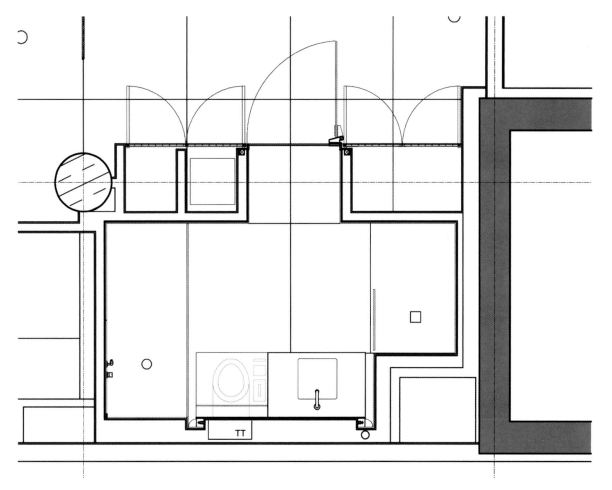

↑ | **Interior view,** Royal Mosa tiles
→ | **Club Sportive,** sauna

Club Sportive
Amsterdam

In the city center of Amsterdam four houses from the 17th to the 19th century were re-developed and converted into a wellness center. Each of the four buildings was given its own color and material – stucco, cement panels, wallpaper, wood – to provide distinct individual atmospheres while moving through the different buildings. In the massive old warehouse, where no sound insulation was necessary, the stucco ceilings were removed to bring the characteristic heavy wooden beams back into view. In the back, a stairwell was created by removing 2x2 beams, bringing daylight to the ground floor and revealing the typical warehouse façade on the inside. The reception, locker rooms and sauna are located in this building.

PROJECT FACTS

Address: Haarlemmer Houttuinen 37–43, Amsterdam, The Netherlands. **Builder-owner:** Club Sportive. **Construction time:** 2004–2006. **Area:** 1,650 m². **Construction costs:** € 1 million. **Project team:** Herman Prast, Ronald Hooft, Martijn Meester, Arjen Bloem.

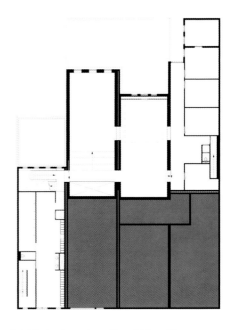

←←| **Interior view,** Royal Mosa tiles
← | **Club Sportive,** sauna
↑ | **Floor plan**
↓ | **Entrance,** locker room

↑ | **Exterior view,** pool on the rooftop
→ | **Façade,** glass roof

Thermae Bath Spa
Bath

Thermae Bath Spa lies within the southwest quadrant of the old walled City of Bath and marks the revitalization of the city's spa quarter. The spa complex comprises one new building – the New Royal Bath – as well as five other buildings that were gently restored. In designing the new-built element of the complex, the architects predominantly employed a limited range of simple geometric forms to achieve a sense of cohesion. The building's dramatic effect derives from the play of light on these forms, creating illusions of transparency and reflection, light and shade, solid and void – ever changing as the sun moves over the south elevation. An elaborate architectural lighting scheme ensures that this interplay of light, form and reflection continues into the evening and through the nighttime hours.

PROJECT FACTS **Address:** Thermae Bath Spa, The Hetling Pump Room, Hot Bath Street, Bath BA1 1SJ, United Kingdom. **Builder-owner:** Bath & North East Somerset Council & Thermae Development Co. **Sponsor:** Millennium Commission. **Opening:** 2006. **Area:** 3,650 ft².

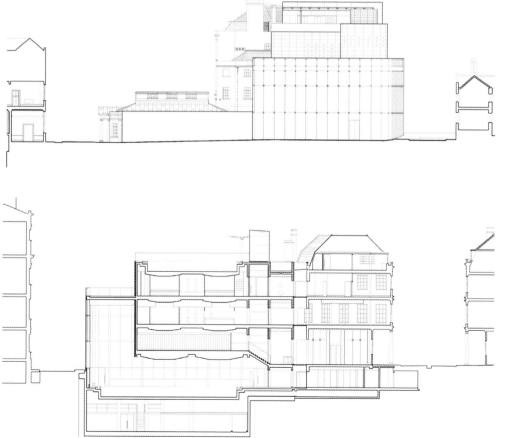

↑ | **Interior view,** spa area
← | **Sections**

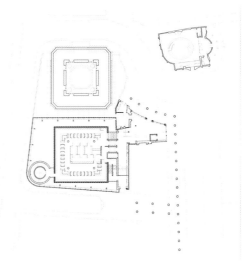

← | **Night view,** entrance
↑ | **Floor plan**
↙ | **Night view,** view of Bath from the pool

Robert D. Henry Architects

↑ | **Treatment room** on the second floor
↓ | **Café, courtyard, local flora**

→ | **Exterior view,** limestone façade

Orient Retreat Spa
Taichung

Previously shadowed by the façades of its mid-rise neighbors, the site at the apex of one of Taiwan's sprawling suburbs on a razed corner lot was transformed to host a more than 2,000 m² flagship spa of Taiwan's largest Spa group, Orient Retreat. The two-story, L-shaped building houses a fully equipped spa, salon, café, and retail boutique. The second floor's monolithic limestone façade floats over the first level's delicate glass enclosure. Before entering the spa one passes through a courtyard composed of bubbling water elements, floating limestone islands, and fragrant local flora. Two perpendicular 20-meter reflecting pools mirror the "L" of the building and glitter with polished river stones. A teak plank glides over the water then turns upwards to form the spa's entry door.

PROJECT FACTS

Address: 4F, No. 81, Sec., 2, An Ho Road, Taichung, Taiwan. **Builder-owner:** The Orient Retreat Spa Group. **Completion:** 05.2004. **Size:** 7,000 ft². **Associate architect:** Archlin, Mr. Lin Tai-You. **Interior designer and consultant:** Design Vanson Company Ltd., Mr. Thomas Wang.

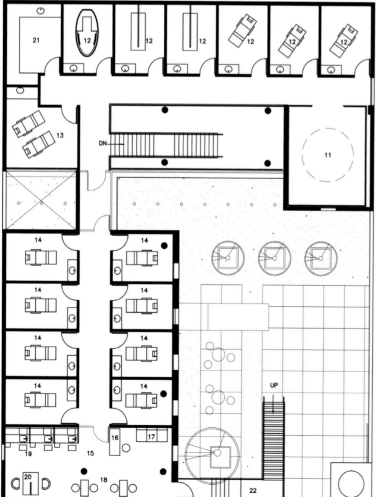

↑ | **Couples treatment room** overlooking water features

← | **Floor plan**

← | Relaxation area
↓ | Sales area

↑ | **Contrast Bath,** double bathtub with different temperatures
↗ | **Face wash,** double sink and underfloor heating in bright yellow
→ | **Shower,** RainSky M without spatial dividers

Dornbracht Tara.Logic
Ritual Bathroom

The Tara.Logic Ritual Bathroom embeds the Tara.Logic fittings by Dornbracht, whose vertical slim design lends them a particularly powerful physique, into an ingenious spatial concept. Panels act as room dividing elements; made of various materials they separate the different zones from each other. The vertical design is transformed into physical activity. The bathroom acts as a private gym in which the body is used as an instrument to achieve physical and mental goals. Based on the Active Spa concept, the six zones of the ritual bathroom are set up like circuit training stations that can be used in a fixed sequence, but also individually.

PROJECT FACTS   **Builder-owner:** Dornbracht. **Area:** 65 m². **Exhibition:** SHK Essen, March 2006. **Product design:** Sieger Design. **Concept and creation:** Meiré und Meiré.

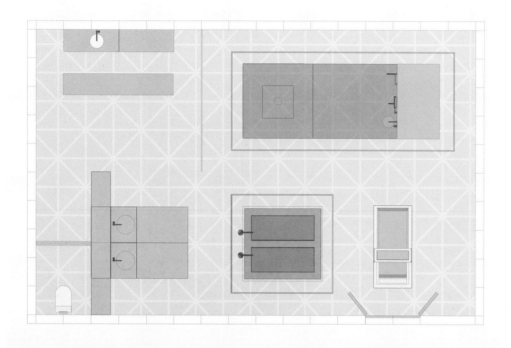

← | **Floor plan**
↙ | **Private gym,** treadmill
→ | **Tara.Logic,** Premium bathroom

Ushi Tamborriello
Innenarchitektur &
Szenenbild

Hamam Trafo
Baden

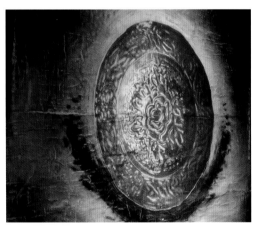

The Hamam, which promises us a refuge from the outside world and a journey to the inside, is located in the landmarked Trafo building. On their journey to the inside, guests are accompanied by colors and surfaces on which the darkness apparently has been deposited in several layers. This includes mystic earthy surface on the walls in different shades of gray and green that clearly show signs of their processing and whose colors reflect those of the steel bearing structures of the landmarked industrial hall, as well as room-high glass walls that control views and insights and that bathe the area in green light. Filtered several times by colored glass and meshed textures, the outside light only enters as a dim memory into the central room of the premises, allowing the floral pattern of the floor to occasionally light up profoundly in the half-light.

A totally new floor covering was developed for the premises, which not only meets the stringent hygienic and anti-skid requirements, but also satisfies all aesthetic demands. The ornaments and patterns of the floor were developed in conjunction with the woodcarving school of Brienz and implemented by the school on location. The venue deliberately frequently breaks with the traditional prototype of the Hamam, reflecting the industrial setting and modernity. What remain are mystic rooms that focus on the same theme – the celebration of a bathing ritual that cleanses body and soul.

↑↑ | **Reception**
↑ | **Detail entrance**
↗ | **Camekan**
→ | **Kurna**

PROJECT FACTS

Address: Brown Boveri Platz 1, 5400 Baden, Switzerland. **Builder-owner:** Genossenschaft Migros Aare. **Opening:** 11.2005. **Construction sum:** approx. CHF 5 million. **Area:** 740 m². **Project management:** S+B Baumanagement AG, Olten. **Project development:** Roger Bernet, rob. d-sign, Aarau.

←← | Kese
↖ | Rain shower
↑ | Rhassoul
← | Sicaklik

↑ | **Exterior view,** projection
→ | **Interior view,** master bathroom

Court-Houses

Miami

In Mies van der Rohe's studio, the "court-house" evolved as a series of glass-enclosed single-story spaces that faced open-air courts and green spaces, all compactly contained within a surrounding rectangular wall. The Miami court-houses were intended as a practical application test of Mies' theoretical investigations, which he never fully implemented in his built work. Two glass-enclosed pavilions – one with living, dining and kitchen spaces, the other with bedrooms – face each other across a central court. The court itself is divided by a lap pool, which is spanned by a concrete bridge. Two additional open courts, heavily planted, provide alternative perspectives of the front and the rear of the houses.

Address: Miami, USA. **Builder-owner:** Terence Riley and John Bennett. **Completion:** 2005.

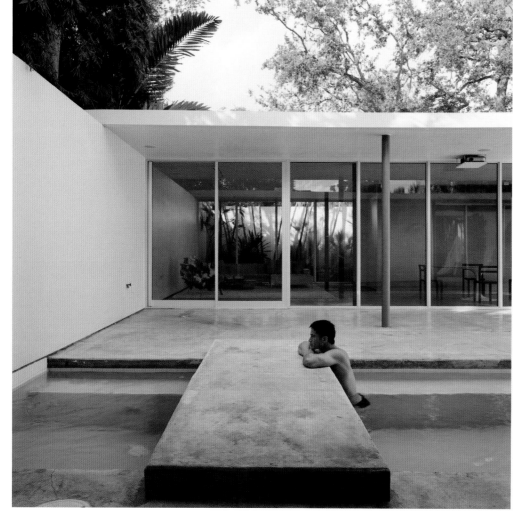

↑← | **Exterior view,** pool in the court

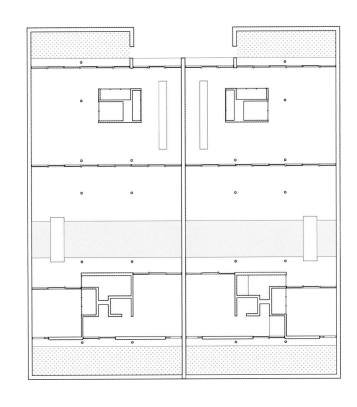

← | **Garden**
↑ | **Floor plan**
↙ | **Bathroom**
↓ | **Lounge,** projection

Klein Dytham architecture

↑ | **Asian bathing tradition**
↓ | **Interior view, façade**

→ | **In the woods,** multi striped color wood siding

Moku Moku Yu

Kobuchizawa

Moku Moku Yu is a timber bathhouse set in the middle of a pine forest in the Risonare resort. Communal bathing is an ancient and venerable tradition in Japan. So too is building in wood. The resulting bathhouse is a cluster of intersecting circular enclosures, immediately inviting aqueous associations with droplets of water or soap bubbles. More significantly, the intersection of spaces serves to blur the usual divisions between inside and outside, and between male and female. Bathers separate by sex at the entrance for undressing and washing, but rejoin again in the outdoor communal bath (konyoku rotenburo). The circles represent the meaning of the bathing ritual in Japan. Rather than responding to the linear functionalist thinking of "take a bath = get clean", this bathhouse provides a series of linked states of being: undress – wash – soak – relax.

PROJECT FACTS

Address: Kobuchizawa, Hokuto-shi, Yamanashi, Japan. **Builder-owner:** Risonare (Hoshino Resort).
Planning and construction time: 11.2004–11.2006. **Area:** 488.60 m². **Structural engineers:** Structured
Environment. **Master builder:** Rinkai Nissan Kensetsu.

↑ | **Interior view,** floor mosaic tiles
←↓ | **Floor plan, section**

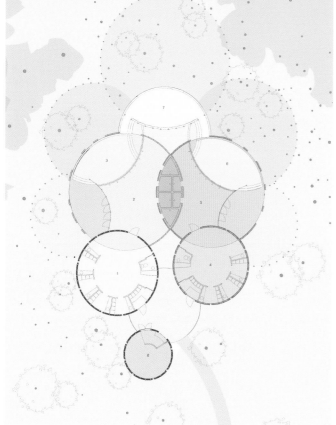

1 changing room (women)
2 shower room (women)
3 bathtub (women)
4 changing room (men)
5 shower room (men)
6 bathtub (men)
7 bathtub (mixed bathing)
8 reception & storage

← | **Outdoor bath,** detail
↓ | **Indoor bath**

↑ | **Steam bath,** glass mosaic by Bisazza
→ | **Detail,** colorful shifting illumination

E'SPA at Gianfranco Ferré
Milan

The recently deceased Gianfranco Ferré descibed his idea of wellness as follows: "An intense pursuit of beauty, that's the essence of my story and my indefatigable research on shapes, colors, materials that adorn the body. Now I go to the very origin of utter luminosity, which becomes a visual sensory pleasure. If fashion is the mere continuous hypothesis of perfecting and enhancing the body, the ultimate truth lies in a genuine feeling of wellness. Thus the body is more important than fashion, which could not even exist without it."

PROJECT FACTS

Address: E'SPA at Gianfranco Ferré, Via Sant'Andrea 15, 20121 Milan, Italy. **Opening:** 05.2003. **Area:** 300 m². **Project management:** Gianfranco Ferré S.p.A. **Consultation:** E'SPA International (UK). **Lighting concept:** Architetto Ezio Riva and Ingegner Massimiliano Rizzo with S.E.I.M.

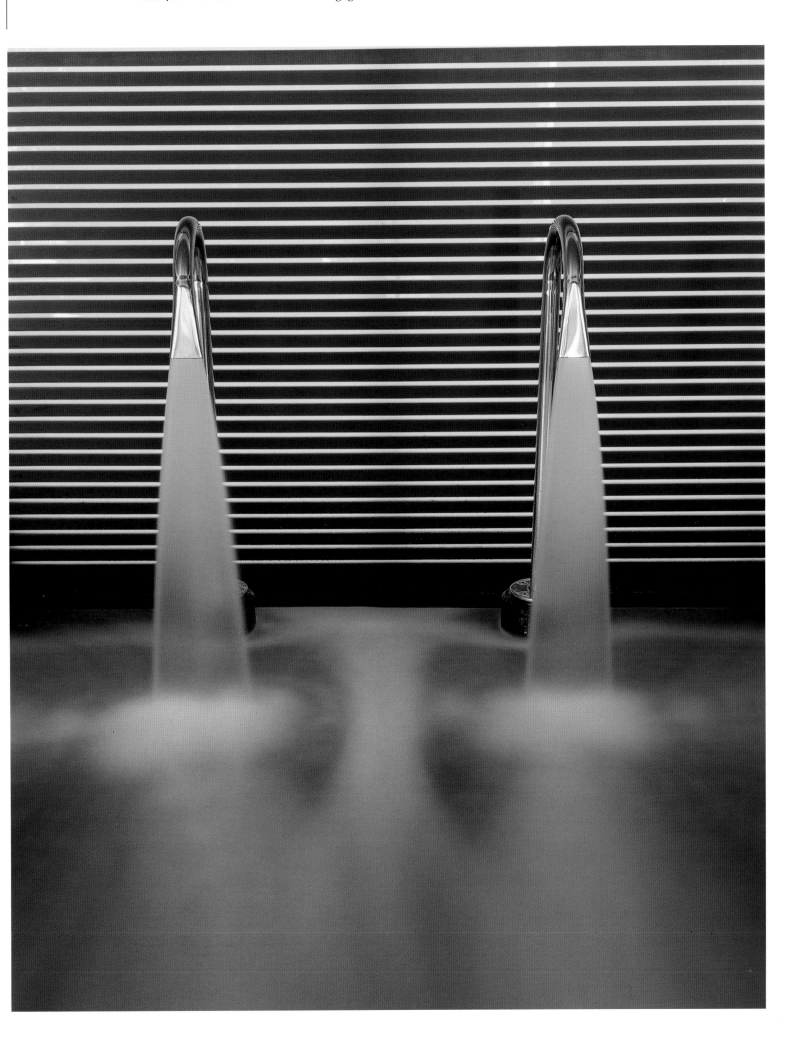

↑← | **Light nuances,** invisible neon tubes use chromotherapy principles

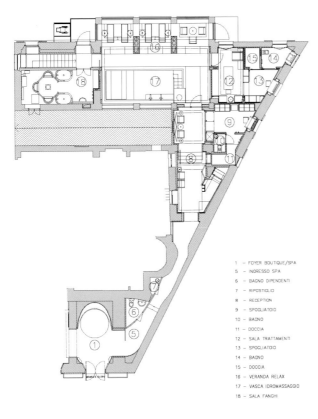

1 – FOYER BOUTIQUE/SPA
5 – INGRESSO SPA
6 – BAGNO DIPENDENTI
7 – RIPOSTIGLIO
8 – RECEPTION
9 – SPOGLIATOIO
10 – BAGNO
11 – DOCCIA
12 – SALA TRATTAMENTI
13 – SPOGLIATOIO
14 – BAGNO
15 – DOCCIA
16 – VERANDA RELAX
17 – VASCA IDROMASSAGGIO
18 – SALA FANGHI

← | **Floor plan**
↙ | **Experience shower,** full gold marks by Bisazza
↓ | **Relaxation room,** ivory leather upholstery

Nalbach + Nalbach
Hon. Prof. Johanne Nalbach

↑ | **Exterior view,** larch façade
↓ | **Spa area,** details

→ | **Interior view,** bathroom

Spa Barn
Seehotel at Neuklostersee, Nakenstorf

Nature was the inspiration for the materials selected for the spa barn. To give the barn construction the greatest possible archaic look, much emphasis was laid on the work carried out on the window openings of the façade and the roof. The window was interpreted as an eye, the façade as a face and the glare shield as an eye lid. The bath area on the ground floor plays with the elements fire, water and earth. The large swimming pool, featuring an open fireplace on the rear side, offers a view of a small birch grove. The adjoined relaxation area, also including an open fireplace, is held completely in white and conveys a sense of lightness and light-heartedness. The overall layout of the spa barn resembles the layout of historic rural barns.

PROJECT FACTS **Address:** Seestrasse 1, 23992 Nakenstorf near Neukloster, Germany. **Builder-owner:** Johanne and Gernot Nalbach, Berlin. **Completion:** 06.2004. **Gross floor area:** approx. 650 m². **Construction sum:** € 1.8 million.

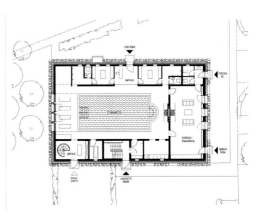

←←| **Swimming pool**
← | **Exterior view**, ivy-covered façade
↑ | **Section**
↙ | **Outdoor spa**, hammock
↓ | **Floor plan**

tects Index

Acquaplan

Via Probello 1
6963 Pregassona-Lugano (Switzerland)
T +41.91.9713131
aeschi@acquaplan.ch
www.acquaplan.ch

→ **148, 194**

Ron Arad

62 Chalk Farm Road
London NW1 8AN (United Kingdom)
T +44.20.72844963
info@ronarad.com
www.ronarad.com

→ **112**

Architecture Research Office LLC

170 Varick Street, 7th Floor
New York, NY 10013 (USA)
T +1.212.6751870
F +1.212.6751645
aro@aro.net
www.aro.net

→ **34**

Jaime Hayon
ArtQuitect

Dolors Granés 79
08440 Cardedeu (Spain)
T +34.93.8444070
artquitect@artquitect.net
www.artquitect.net

→ **152**

Behles & Jochimsen

Kurfürstendamm 11
10719 Berlin (Germany)
T +49.30.325948360
F +49.30.325948380
eingang@behlesjochimsen.de
www.behlesjochimsen.de

→ **168**

Titus Bernhard Architekten

Gögginger Strasse 105a
86199 Augsburg (Germany)
T +49.821.5996050
F +49.821.59960510
info@berhardarchitekten.com
www.titus-bernhard.de

→ **38, 114**

Mario Botta

Via Ciani 16
6904 Lugano (Switzerland)
T +41.91.9728625
F +41.91.9701454
info@botta.ch
www.botta.ch

→ **76**

Dirkjan Broekhuizen
Interieurarchitect BNI

Nieuweweg 1
6871 CA Renkum (The Netherlands)
T +31.317.319536
F +31.317.319539
info@dirkjanbroekhuizen.com
www.dirkjanbroekhuizen.com

→ **68, 160**

Joseph Caspari Architect

8 rue de Miromesnil
75008 Paris (France)
T +33.662036148
joseph.caspari@ orange.fr

→ **64**

Yves Collet

6 avenue Jean Jaures
92240 Malakoff (France)
T +33.1.40929821
F +33.1.40921254
collet-burger@wanadoo.fr

→ **88, 200**

Crepain Binst Architecture

Vlaanderenstraat 6
2000 Antwerpen (Belgium)
T +32.3.2136161
F +32.3.2136162
mail@crepainbinst.be
www.crepainbinst.be

Carl D'Aquino & Francine D'Aquino of D'Aquino Monaco

214 West 29th Street
New York, NY 10001 (USA)
T +1.212.9299787
F +1.212.9299225
monarch@daquinomonaco.com
www.daquinomonaco.com

D E SIGNSTUDIO
REGINA DAHMEN-INGENHOVEN

Plange Mühle 1
40221 Düsseldorf (Germany)
T +49.211.3010101
F +49.211.3010131
info@drdi.de
www.drdi.de

Jeff Etelamaki Design Studio

55 Washington Street, Suite 253B
Brooklyn, NY 11201 (USA)
T +1.718.6663152
F +1.718.5046455
info@je-designstudio.com
je-designstudio.com

Gianfranco Ferré

Via Pontaccio 21
20121 Milan (Italy)
T +39.02.76017526
F +39.02.721341
www.gianfrancoferre.com

Finkeldey + Uetrecht
nexus product design

Muerfeldstrasse 22
33719 Bielefeld (Germany)
T +49.521.333352
F +49.521.333382
info@nexusproductdesign.de
www.nexusproductdesign.de

Uwe Bernd Friedemann

Rathenauplatz 21
50674 Cologne (Germany)
T +49.221.325883
UBF@UweBerndFriedemann.de
www.UweBerndFriedemann.de

Otello Giorgio Gatto

Marisstraat 8–10
6165 AS Geleen (The Netherlands)
T +31.46.4376340
F +31.46.4376340
info@gatto.nl
www.gatto.nl

Jacques Garcia

212 rue de Rivoli
75001 Paris (France)
T +33.1.42974870
F +33.1.42974810

gmp – Architekten von Gerkan, Marg und Partner

Elbchaussee 139
22763 Hamburg (Germany)
T +49.40.881510
F +49.40.88151177
Hamburg-E@gmp-architekten.de
www.gmp-architekten.de

GRAFT Architekten
Lars Krückeberg
Wolfram Putz
Thomas Willemeit

Heidestrasse 50
10557 Berlin (Germany)
T +49.30.24047985
F +49.30.24047987
berlin@graftlab.com
www.graftlab.com

Grimshaw

57 Clerkenwell Road
London EC1M 5NG (United Kingdom)
T +44.20.72914141
F +44.20.72914194
info@grimshaw-architects.com
www.grimshaw-architects.com

→ **230**

Zaha Hadid

10 Bowling Green Lane
London EC1R 0BQ (United Kingdom)
T +44.20.72535147
F +44.20.72518322
info@zaha-hadid.com
www.zaha-hadid.com

→ **20**

Robert D. Henry Architects

37 East 18th Street, 10th Floor
New York, NY 10003 (USA)
T +1.212.5334145
F +1.212.5989028
info@rdh-architects.com
www.rdh-architects.com

→ **176, 234**

K/R Architects

526 West 26th Street #9a
New York, NY 10001 (USA)
T +1.212.6459210
F +1.212.6459211
jk@krnyc.com
www.krnyc.com

→ **246**

kbm architekten

Fettstrasse 7a
20357 Hamburg (Germany)
T +49.40.43278966
F +49.40.43278968
office@kbm-architekten.de
www.kbm-architekten.de

→ **90**

Klein Dytham architecture

AD Bldg 2F, 1-15-7 Hiroo, Shibuya-ku
Tokyo 150 – 0012 (Japan)
T +81.03.57952277
F +81.03.5795.2276
kda@klein-dytham.com
www.klein-dytham.com

→ **250**

G. Hakan Kulahci
Artmim IC Mimari Tasarim

Organize Sahayi Bölgesi 1, Cd. ART-MIM Binasi
Antalya (Turkey)
T +90.242.3165500
F +90.242.3165505
info@artmim.com.tr
www.artmim.com.tr

→ **218**

Licht 01

Fettstrasse 7a
20357 Hamburg (Germany)
T +49.40.43095323
F +49.40.43095329
info@licht01.de
www.licht01.de

→ **202**

Loodszeven Interieurarchitecten

Hertogsingel 50
6214 AE Maastricht (The Netherlands)
T +31.6.10399322
F +31.6.10318183
info@loodszeven.nl
www.loodszeven.nl

→ **30**

Lykouria Design London

39–41 North Road
London N7 9DP (United Kingdom)
T +44.207.6970082
info@jahnlykouria.com
www.lykouria.com

→ **16, 224**

Javier Mariscal & Fernando Salas
Estudio Mariscal

Bellaires 30–38
08019 Barcelona (Spain)
T +34.933.036940
F +34.932.662244
javier@mariscal.com
www.mariscal.com

→ 46

Studio Massaud

T +33.140.095414
F +33.140.090816
studio@massaud.com
www.massaud.com

→ 190

Julie Mathias

2 Leswin Place Unit HQ
London N16 7NJ (United Kingdom)
T +44.20.71681184
julie@wokmedia.com
www.wokmedia.com

→ 144

Meiré und Meiré

Lichtstrasse 26–28
50825 Cologne (Germany)
info@meireundmeire.de
www.meireundmeire.de

→ 56, 238

Nalbach + Nalbach
Hon. Prof. Johanne Nalbach

Rheinstrasse 44–46, Aufgang 3, 2. OG
12161 Berlin (Germany)
T +49.30.8590830
F +49.30.8511210
buero@nalbach-architekten.de
www.nalbach-architekten.de

→ 258

Nieberg Architect

Waterloostrasse 1
30169 Hanover (Germany)
T +49.511.1696601
F +49.511.1696602
mail@nieberg-architect.de
www.nieberg-architect.de

→ 102, 136

Fabio Novembre

Via Perugino 26
20135 Milan (Italy)
T +39.02.504104
F +39.02.502375
info@novembre.it
www.novembre.it

→ 126, 206

Jean Nouvel

10 cité d'Angoulême
75011 Paris (France)
T +33.01.49238383
F +33.01.43148115
info@jeannouvel.fr
www.jeannouvel.fr

→ 140

Giovanni Pagani
Maurizio di Mauro

Via Emilia
14 Ponte Enza – Reggio Emilia (Italy)
T +39.0522.902145
F +39.0522.671826
studio@paganidimauro.com
www.paganidimauro.com

→ 52

plajer & franz studio

Erkelenzdamm 59/61
10999 Berlin (Germany)
F +49.30.6165580
F +49.30.61655829
studio@plajer-franz.de
www.plajer-franz.de

→ 132

Plan2Plus
Ralf Peter Knobloch
Ursula Regina Förster

Friedrich-Herschel-Strasse 3
81679 Munich (Germany)
T +49.89.61209090
F +49.89.61209092
info@plan2plus.de
www.plan2plus.de

→ 40

Plasma Studio

Unit 51 – Regents Studios
8 Andrews Road
London E8 4QN (United Kingdom)
T +44.207.8129875
F +44.870.4865563
info@plasmastudio.com
www.plasmastudio.com

→ 214

PrastHooft

Kraijenhoffstraat 32
1018 RL Amsterdam (The Netherlands)
T +31.6.26748545
F +31.20.5289645
prast@prasthooft.nl
www.prasthooft.nl

→ 226

Andrée Putman

83 avenue Demferd-Rochereau
75014 Paris (France)
T +33.01.55428855
archi@andreeputman.com
www.andreeputman.com

→ 118

Schletterer Wellness & Spa Design
Stefan Ghetta

Strass 190
6261 Strass im Zillertal (Austria)
T +43.5244.62005.526
F +43.5244.62005.50
office@schletterer.com
www.schletterer.com

→ 24

Michael Schmidt
code.2.design

Ludwigstrasse 59
70176 Stuttgart (Germany)
T +49.711.50531350
F +49.711.50531355
info@code2design.de
www.code2design.de

→ 74

Wieki Somers

Nieuwe haven 91
3116 AB Schiedam (The Netherlands)
T +31.10.2460699
F +31.10.2460698
info@wiekisomers.com
www.wiekisomers.com

→ 124

Ushi Tamborriello
Innenarchitektur & Szenenbild

Holzstrasse 33
80469 Munich (Germany)

Landstrasse 1
5415 Rieden / Baden (Switzerland)
ushi@tamborriello.de
www.tamborriello.de

→ 198, 242

Terrazzo Werkstatt Regensburg
Michael Dorrer

Geiersberg Weg 2
93059 Regensburg (Germany)
T +49.941.4646191
terrazzoregensburg@t-online.de

→ 60

Matteo Thun

Via Appiani 9
20121 Milan (Italy)
T +39.02.655691
F +39.02.6570646
info@matteothun.com
www.matteothun.com

→ 12, 210

Marcel Wanders Studio

Westerstraat 187
1015 MA Amsterdam (The Netherlands)
T +31.20.4221339
F +31.20.6815056
pr@marcelwanders.com
www.marcelwanders.com

→ 172

Büro Wehberg

Holländische Reihe 13a
22765 Hamburg (Germany)
T +49.40.39909866
F +49.40.39909867
info@buero-wehberg.de
www.buero-wehberg.de

→ 106

Markus Wespi Jérôme de Meuron Architekten BSA

6578 Caviano (Switzerland)
T +41.91.7941773
F +41.91.7941773
info@wespidemeuron.ch
www.wespidemeuron.ch

→ 94

YES-architecture

Marion Wicher
Griesgasse 10
8020 Graz (Austria)
T +43.316.764891
F +43.316.7648998
wicher@yes-architecture.com

Ruth Bergtold
Lindwurmstrasse 71
80337 Munich (Germany)
T +49.89.44409933
F +49.89.44409935
bergtold@yes-architecture.com
www.yes-architecture.com

→ 156

PICTURE CREDITS

More INTERIORS

The interior design of recent years stands out above all for its original use of materials. Classic building materials, such as concrete, stone and wood, are now being employed in a variety of new ways and the novel combination of the design elements colour, fabric, glass and light creates different interior ambiences.

Both volumes present a unique selection of over 120 notable designed interiors – ranging from private residences to small businesses and major public buildings. Architects, interior designers and artists demonstrate how the personality of a given space can be decisively formed through an innovative interplay of materials. The projects included here are presented in such a way as to provide the reader with a source both of inspiration and information, taking them on a spectacular tour of unusual designed spaces.

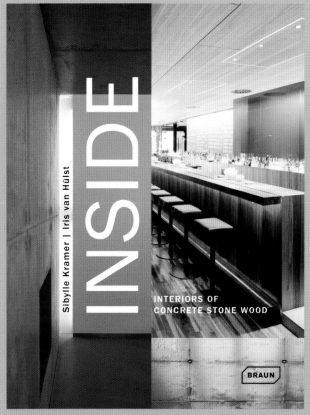

Sibylle Kramer | Iris van Hülst

INSIDE

INTERIORS OF
CONCRETE STONE WOOD

BRAUN

ISBN 978-3-938780-19-0

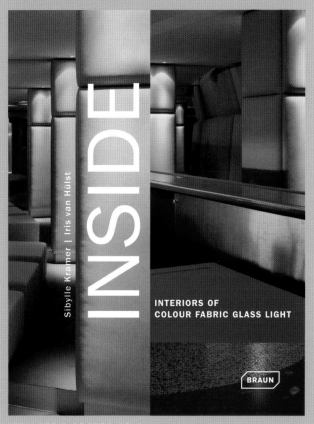

Sibylle Kramer | Iris van Hülst

INSIDE

INTERIORS OF
COLOUR FABRIC GLASS LIGHT

BRAUN

ISBN 978-3-938780-40-4

BRAUN

IMPRINT

The Deutsche Bibliothek is registering this publication in the Deutsche Nationalbibliographie; detailed bibliographical information can be found on the Internet at http://dnb.ddb.de

ISBN 978-3-938780-39-8

© 2008 by Verlagshaus Braun
www.verlagshaus-braun.de

1st edition 2008

Selection of projects: Sibylle Kramer
Project coordination: Marc von Reth
Editorial staff: Anna Hinc
Translation: Cosima Talhouni
Graphic concept: ON Grafik | Tom Wibberenz
Layout: Michaela Prinz
Reproduction: Bild1Druck GmbH, Berlin